JOSEPH LOCKE

JOSEPH LOCKE

Civil Engineer and Railway Builder
1805 - 1860

Anthony Burton

PEN & SWORD
TRANSPORT

First published in Great Britain in 2017 by
PEN & SWORD TRANSPORT
an imprint of
Pen & Sword Books Ltd,
47 Church Street,
Barnsley,
South Yorkshire,
S70 2AS

A CIP record for this book is available from the British Library.

ISBN 978 1 47387 229 5

Printed and Bound in UK by TJ International.

Pen & Sword Books Ltd incorporates the Imprints of Pen & Sword Aviation, Pen & Sword Maritime, Pen & Sword Military, Wharncliffe Local History, Pen & Sword Select, Pen & Sword Military Classics and Leo Cooper.

For a complete list of Pen & Sword titles please contact
Pen & Sword Books Limited
47 Church Street, Barnsley, South Yorkshire, S70 2AS, England

E-mail: enquiries@pen-and-sword.co.uk
Website: www.pen-and-sword.co.uk

CONTENTS

PREFACE

To call Joseph Locke the forgotten engineer would be quite wrong, but he is certainly not as well known as some of his contemporaries. He deserves to be better known, and in this book I have tried to show exactly why he should be honoured as one of the great railway pioneers, a pivotal figure in establishing the basis of our present railway system. There is not a great deal in the following pages about his personal life, especially in his later years, simply because it seems the information is not available. As a young man he wrote entertaining and chatty letters, but if he continued doing so into later years, then they have not survived. What remains tends to be formal and business-like but often illuminating. This may be a disappointment to some readers, but this is the life of a man who devoted far more time to his profession than he did to private pleasures. And it is his life as an engineer that is being celebrated here.

It is altogether appropriate that this book should be published by a company based in Barnsley, the town where Locke grew up and which he always held in great affection. I hope the citizens of that town will feel that this book does their local hero justice.

Anthony Burton
Stroud

Chapter One

THE LOCKE FAMILY

Joseph Locke's family worked in the heart of the industry that was central to the industrial revolution sweeping through Britain in the second half of the eighteenth century. They were employed at collieries, and it was in mining that steam power was developed, at first simply for pumping out water to enable miners to go ever deeper underground, then later to power machinery. Until 1800, development of steam power had been hampered by James Watt's all-embracing patent, but when that patent expired in 1800, the way was open to find new ways of using this power. It was the Cornish mining engineer Richard Trevithick who broke with Watt's view that the only safe way to get more power was to keep pressure low and build ever bigger engines. Trevithick used high-pressure steam to construct powerful small engines. His first attempts were portable engines that could be towed to where they were needed by horses, but in 1801 he built a locomotive that could move itself along the road. One big difficulty he faced was steering the machine – his prototype only survived a few days before being run off the road and left to simmer, resulting in a boiler explosion that ended its career. Exactly when that problem found a unique solution is open to question, but we can say with certainty that in July 1804, Trevithick gave the first public demonstration of a steam locomotive running on a railed track. The railway age had been born – and just over a year later, on 9 August 1805, Joseph Locke made his appearance in the world. The family could hardly have guessed that the event that had taken place in South Wales would define the future of the newborn child.

Although family connections with coal mining went back several generations, the Lockes were not face workers. The men had mainly supervisory positions. Joseph's grandfather was a colliery manager at White Lane in what is now a suburb of Sheffield, but an area with a mining history going back at least as far as the sixteenth century. He was soon to get an even more important position as coal viewer for the Duke of Norfolk's extensive estates. He was able to use his influence to help his sons find suitable jobs in the industry. William Locke, Joseph's father was born in 1770 and in 1798 he was bankman at Water Row colliery near Newburn in Northumberland. This was a task, according to Joseph Devey in his biography of Joseph Locke (1862), that was comparatively straightforward. 'For this nothing was required but an intimate acquaintance with the three rudiments of education, and a reputation for impartial and judicial integrity.' It was not quite that simple. The miners sent up tubs of coal, known as corves, each marked with the insignia of the gang who had filled it. They were paid on the basis of the number of full corves sent up per day. This sounds a foolproof system, but the bankman was required not only to enter the details but also to assess whether or not the corves were completely filled and to check whether other material had been included. If he judged any to be less than the required standard, then the men got nothing – the owners, of course, got an almost full corve for free. One miner in a Durham colliery recorded sending up seven corves and only getting paid for three. Being a bankman never won anyone a prize in the popularity stakes: but William Locke was not a man to court popularity.

He was joined at Water Row in 1798 by a seventeen-year-old, who had also followed his father into the mining industry. The young man had already shown himself to have great mechanical aptitude, and in spite of his youth he was given the very responsible job of plugman for one of the steam engines, used to pump water from the mine. He had to check that the pumps were working efficiently; on occasions, one of the suction holes would become uncovered when water levels dropped. This allowed air in, preventing the pump from working. When that happened, the man had to go and plug the hole – hence the title. His name was George Stephenson.

Samuel Smiles, in his biography of George and Robert Stephenson (1862), tells a story of the two men. Young George was sometimes allowed to act as brakeman by Bill Coe, the man in charge of a small winding engine, used to haul coal from the pit bottom to the surface. This was a skilled job, requiring great accuracy in operation, as the brakeman had to rely on indicators to show the position of the cage in the shaft:

Coe was, however, opposed by several of the other workmen – one of whom, a banksman named William Locke, went so far as to stop the working of the pit because Stephenson had been called in to the brake. But one day as Mr. Charles Nixon, the manager of the pit, was observed approaching, Coe adopted an expedient which put a stop to the opposition. He called upon Stephenson to 'come into the brakehouse, and take hold of the machine.' Locke, as usual, sat down and the working of the pit was stopped. When requested by the manager to give an explanation, he said that 'young Stephenson couldn't brake, and, what was more, never would learn, he was so clumsy.' Mr Nixon, however, ordered Locke to go on with the work, which he did, and Stephenson, after some further practice, acquired the art of braking.

This would certainly suggest that relations between Locke and Stephenson were a good deal less than friendly but, as this is the only written account describing any sort of connection between the two at this time, it has to be taken seriously. There are two things to note. The first is that this was written more than half a century after the event, so that one can safely assume that the spoken words quoted are an invention. Was the story itself true in general? Smiles was notorious for putting his heroes in the best possible light – this story uses the apparently mean-minded Locke as a foil for the enthusiastic Stephenson. It may well be that Locke, who as it will appear, was a stickler for the strict letter of the law, raised an objection to an untrained lad being given such a responsible job, but not perhaps in quite the terms Smiles uses. To set against this account is the fact that although we know little about their relations while they were both at the same pit, we do know that they were on excellent terms later in life. As Stephenson was notoriously not a man to forget an insult, it can be assumed that Smiles' story comes highly coloured to increase the drama. Since George Stephenson was to play a crucial role in Joseph's early career, it is just as well that the incident, whatever the details may have been, did nothing to permanently sour relations between the great engineer and William Locke.

Our best character sketch of William Locke comes from his grandson, Arthur Austin, who described him in his old age in his autobiography published in 1911. Austin certainly had good reason to look favourably on his mother's side of the family, as it was his uncle Joseph who bequeathed him the money that enabled him to leave a career in law to become a full-time poet. He was to become Britain's least read poet laureate, remembered chiefly, if not entirely fairly, for a terrible couplet, written about an illness of Edward VII:

Flash'd from his bed, the electric tidings came.
He is not much better, he is much the same.

Not, one imagines, the lines he would have chosen to go down to posterity. He did, however, give a neat little cameo of his grandfather, which goes a long way to explaining the little fracas between Locke and Stephenson.

William Locke was a Roman Catholic, but not perhaps typical. Austin described him as 'that extraordinary thing, a Roman Catholic Puritan.' He married Esther Teesdale, who converted to Catholicism, and who became 'the mere perfectly happy shadow of his will.' She found him a man not much given to fripperies, and as Austin described him strict to the point of obsession: 'A man of scrupulous honour and severe integrity.' These are no doubt admirable qualities, but there was a downside. 'It can hardly be necessary to add that such austere righteousness was accompanied by commensurate narrowness of mind and judgement. When, after her marriage, my Mother occasionally went to concerts and dances, he observed, "I wonder where Mary expects to go when she dies."' His severity extended to his reading matter, mainly serious works, and one may guess his poetic tastes by what he always declared was the finest line in all English poetry. It comes from Alexander Pope's long poem, *An Essay on Man*, not the best known line:

The proper study of mankind is man.

But a line that was the template for his life:

An honest man's the noblest work of God.

Austin knew him only in old age, when he had retired from his professional life, but he was never idle, spending long hours in his garden. And his views seem never to have altered about what constituted real, honest work, as the young Austin discovered. 'On one occasion he asked me what were my chief studies at school; and as land surveying was not among them, I could see that his conclusion was that I was not being educated at all.'

William Locke was noted for his scrupulous honesty and unbending morality: traits he expected to find in everyone else he met, and when, inevitably, he failed to find his expectations were met, he acted accordingly. In 1802, his father arranged a far better position for him as overseer for a colliery at Attercliffe. At the time, Attercliffe was a self-contained village on the outskirts of Sheffield, beside the River Don. It was not itself a mining village, but mainly notable for its orchards, old windmill and less appealingly, its gibbet. There was, however, a well established local industry, mainly making penknives, and the heavy industry of Sheffield itself was in sight of the village common. Nevertheless it was an attractive place to live, and William seemed well settled, with a good job and comfortable home.

All went well for a time, but in William Locke's life there was always something lurking just over the horizon, waiting to test his moral rectitude. The actual details of what went wrong are not altogether clear, but Devey, in his biography of Joseph Locke, makes it clear that William had been told that if there was a change in the partnership running the mine, then he would be given a share of the profits. The change took place, but William's share never materialised. Perhaps the new partners saw no reason to be bound by promises made by their predecessors, perhaps there was a misunderstanding, but whatever the reason, William took the high moral ground. A promise had been made; the promise had been broken. He could not work for such men. He quit and found a new post near Huddersfield at the colliery belonging to Sir John Ramsden.

The Ramsden family were public benefactors who did a great deal to develop Huddersfield. Sir John Ramsden, while still a minor, persuaded his legal guardians to allow him to finance a canal that would link the town to the River Calder. Today, known either as Sir John Ramsden's Canal or Huddersfield Broad Canal, it is still in use, forming with the Huddersfield Narrow Canal part of a trans-Pennine route. So William was now joining a progressive, forward-thinking establishment. He had a moderately comfortable house in Attercliffe with a large garden where he could raise his own produce. The early nineteenth century was a difficult time for all industrial workers. Due to the Combination Acts it was illegal to form trade unions to fight for better pay and conditions – though the law said nothing about employers getting together to set pay and prices. Three years after William went to the colliery near Huddersfield there was a strike and William inevitably saw himself as the champion of his employer's interests and as an upholder of the law.

It was a situation that might have been resolved by negotiation and compromise, but William called on the law to prosecute those who were considered ringleaders for illegally organising the strike. As a result one man was sent to Wakefield gaol.

In time the dispute was settled, but the ill feeling towards William Locke was so fierce that the men refused to work while he was still in charge. According to Devey, Sir John regarded William as his 'faithful and valued servant', but perhaps he was not that highly regarded after all. Sir John agreed that Locke must go. At the heart of the whole situation was, once again, William Locke's unbending devotion to what he saw as being the right action; and he would do what was right regardless of any possible consequences for himself. So, once again, he was out of a job, but only temporarily. The agent at a colliery in Barnsley was killed in an accident. One of the partners was a Mr Clayton, who also had shares in Kippax Colliery, near Leeds, in which William's brother John also had shares. It was a fortunate coincidence, and William was duly offered the job, and the family moved to Barnsley. It was here that William's son Joseph would be raised and educated and it was to be the town to which he always retained a close connection.

Arriving at his new position, William found a wretched state of affairs, with workings badly in need of maintenance, but with the books showing a niggardly profit of a mere £200 a year. It was a classical dilemma: without extensive work the pit could not show a profit, but without a profit there was no money to pay for the work. William began the task of making steady improvements, providing sufficient savings and increased efficiency to make money for the essential repairs and maintenance work. Once those were well under way, the results were immediately apparent in increased revenue. He managed to turn £200 a year into a healthier return of £1200. There was even a turn in his own fortunes. His father died and he was able to take over the additional position of coal viewer to the Duke of Norfolk. It was the one job that he was able to keep for the rest of his life. Readers will not perhaps be too surprised to discover that after a good start, things started to go wrong at Barnsley.

One of the partners at the colliery cast some sort of doubt about William's management of affairs. William demanded that the other absentee partner come over to check things out for himself. He arrived:

the books and the works were scrutinised and William was vindicated. It was agreed that he had done a splendid job, but those scruples were brought out yet again. One partner had cast doubt on his work, possibly even questioned his honesty; he would leave as soon as a new agent could be appointed. The partner who had caused the problem in the first place was to apologise later, and even to consult William on a few occasions, but the harm had been done. It was as well that the Norfolk job had materialised at the same time.

Now William, perhaps tired of what he regarded as ill treatment and insults from former employers, decided to invest his savings, such as they were, in a pit of his own in Barnsley. But trouble, as ever, dogged his efforts. This time there was a dispute with another local, who claimed that the workings were having an adverse effect on a watercourse on his land. Perhaps it could all have been settled amicably with negotiation and compromise but that, of course, was never going to be William's way. He went to law. Going to law is almost invariably a course of action fraught with uncertainty and likely to cost more than it gains. It is not a course to be taken lightly, and should perhaps be avoided altogether if the man on the opposite side is also a lawyer, which was the case here. William Locke ploughed on anyway, with the inevitable consequence: he lost his case and lost his pit.

It was to be the last of his misfortunes. In 1832, now in his sixties, William inherited another post as coal viewer for Lord Stourton. He had pits between Leeds and Wakefield, and Locke and family moved to the area, first to Sandal Magna, a spot now on the outskirts of Leeds, then to Rothwell Haigh. Rothwell itself was then a pleasant, small market town and the house was an attractive one in substantial grounds. The house shared its name with the local pit that was later to be renamed Victoria Pit, and the name Rothwell Haigh lives on in a local primary school. His work was not onerous, involving no more than three or four trips down the pit each year to check on the amounts of coal that had been won. That did not mean he led an idle life; idleness was not part of his creed. He was up early each day, working in the grounds, which contained attractive areas for leisure and an extensive kitchen garden. His working day was determined by dawn and sunset, not the clock. As his wife remarked, he had 'no moderation'.

There was much to admire in the life of William Locke. He was a devout Catholic, who was known to travel miles to church if one was not to be found close at hand and took the church's teachings as the guiding force in his life. He was scrupulously honest and never shirked his duty. Devey tells a story from Barnsley days, when there were fears that the pit was full of firedamp, methane gas, the cause of many explosions that caused huge loss of life in collieries. Where others were reluctant, he was the man who took it upon himself to investigate the problem: personal safety was less important than duty. This was very admirable, but his character clearly made him an uncomfortable person to deal with: rigid and uncompromising. His early biographer Devey paints a picture of a man more sinned against than sinning, but when one finds him falling out with his colleagues and fellow workers time and time again, one cannot help feeling that the faults were not all on one side. But, however many problems he had at work, his home life seems to have been a happy one. In spite of his occasional grumblings about frivolities, he appears to have been a devoted husband and father to their children. Altogether, there were to be seven children, four boys and three girls, and the sixth of the brood was Joseph.

Chapter Two
EARLY LIFE

Joseph's temperament was, it seems, very different from that of his father. His biographer Devey had the opportunity to talk to his surviving brothers and sisters, and they all spoke of a lively, mischievous young boy. He was fond of telling stories, practical jokes and teasing his sisters, but got on well with his siblings, especially the teased sisters. He was less popular with his father, who disapproved of his antics and the boy was apparently frequently sent up to his room for 'being too forward and positive for anything'.

The family moved to Barnsley when Joseph was 5-years-old. The town is an ancient one, being mentioned in the Domesday Book. It might have been just an ordinary country town, its importance depending on the annual fair and weekly market, granted by a charter in 1249, but once it was found to be sitting on an extensive coalfield its character changed. By the early seventeenth century, glass making had been added to mining and in the eighteenth century it developed an extensive linen-weaving industry. Its open spaces and commons disappeared when an Enclosure Act was passed in 1777, so that by the time the Locke family arrived it had already become what Alfred Austin called 'that grimy town'.

Joseph's education began at Barnsley Grammar School, an institution that apparently offered no more than the basic requirements of drumming in the three Rs with the frequent assistance of the cane and the cuff round the ear. According to one of his sisters, Joseph was a less than assiduous scholar, 'though she used to be amazed at the neglect with which he treated his tasks up to the last moment, the concentrated determination with which he then attacked, and the accurate determination with which he finished them, even these did not save him from having to endure …those brutal assaults which a more understanding age condemns and disallows.' In those days, grammar school education had to be paid for, so that it was unlikely that his father, given his views on academic subjects, would have been willing to let him try for any form of higher education. In any case, for a boy who seemed destined for a practical career, there was very little on offer. Although some countries made provision for studying subjects such as engineering – the French had their École des Ponts at Chaussés in the eighteenth century – nothing similar existed in Britain. The English universities, had they been within the families' means, would not have helped, though he might have fared better in Scotland, where educational ideas were more progressive than they were south of the border. The engineer John Rennie caustically remarked that 'when a young man has been three or four years at the University of Oxford or Cambridge, he cannot, without much difficulty, turn himself to the practical part of civil engineering.' There was only one route forward, so at the age of thirteen Joseph left school, and was apprenticed to William Stobart at Pelaw, just south of Newcastle. The placement was again using family connections, for Stobart was one of the Duke of Norfolk's agents and a highly respected colliery viewer.

Stobart seems to have enjoyed a very friendly relationship with his young pupil and though as rough as many men were who worked in that industry, he always had a pious word when he and Joseph set off down the pit: 'Now, Joe, God go wi' us.' This is not surprising, for miners at that time knew all too well the dangers of the job. The pit was very close to Felling Colliery where, in 1812, a disastrous accident resulted in ninety-two lives being lost, and the following year disaster struck again when twenty-two died.

Things went well between master and apprentice for a couple of years until one of those rows developed that seemed to plague the Locke family. It appears trivial enough. He was required to take the family letter bag to the post, which involved a pony ride. For some reason he took offence: either it was beneath the dignity of a would-be colliery viewer to be seen as a mere post boy, or perhaps he resented being used by the family as an unpaid servant. Whatever the reason, it soured relationships and Joseph returned to Barnsley.

Perhaps on reflection, Joseph realised that he had behaved in a rather petty, foolish manner. Many years later, Stobart and his daughter were travelling by stagecoach when an apparently highly respectable gentleman treated them with great courtesy. It was only after he had left the coach and they had asked the guard who the gentleman was that they discovered it was Joseph Locke.

His sisters welcomed him back, but his parents were less enthusiastic about having a hungry, unemployed teenager at the family table. William heard about a position with a young land surveyor in Rochdale, hired a gig and drove his son across the Pennines and deposited him with his new master. The surveyor turned out to have only just set up in business, could not afford to pay for a nurse for the latest addition to the family and the main occupation for the boy was to be baby sitting. Two weeks of that was enough. He left Rochdale and walked the thirty-odd miles back to Barnsley. As always he had an entertaining story for his sisters; striding across Blackstone Edge, a labourer shouted after him, 'Eh! But thou art a swaggering fou!' The parents were not amused. Two positions had been found for the boy, and still he was back living with them. The only option left seemed to be to find young Joseph work at the colliery his father was managing. But it was comparatively menial office work that occupied most of his time and when there was nothing much there for him, he was sent out 'leading' coal, in effect going around the town with a horse and cart, selling coal to the locals. The boy who had objected to being seen carrying the post, was even less enthralled at the idea of being seen as a door-to-door coalman. He tried to keep this lowly employment from those who knew him, by hiding whenever anyone came in sight or even paying a man threepence to lead the horse in areas where he was known. He was intensely miserable and later recalled lying down in a field and 'crying like a child.'

Joseph Locke does not seem to have had the sort of temperament to dwell too much on the miseries of life. He was still the boy who amused his family with stories and anecdotes and was always on the lookout for new amusements. On one occasion he entered a raffle hoping to win a fiddle, but it went to another man who, as is so often the way in such things, had no use for a violin. They agreed that if Joseph fetched his water from the pump for a while, he could have the fiddle, which he duly did, though there seems to be very little evidence of his musical talents. Being at home again meant having to do his share of family chores, including looking after the cow his father had bought. It was a task he loathed and when his father decided to sell the animal, Joseph recalled he got out of bed with more enthusiasm than he'd shown for months. These were not happy times for the eighteen-year-old and with no future prospects he is said to have considered emigrating. Everything changed, however, with a letter that arrived for William Locke from Killingworth Colliery dated 31 March 1823:

Dear Sir – From the great elapse of time since I saw you, you will hardly know that such a man is in the land of the living.

I fully expected to have seen you about two years ago, as I passed through Barnsley on my way to South Wales; but being informed you were not at home, I did not call. I expect to be in London in the course of a fortnight or three weeks, when I shall do myself the pleasure of calling, either in going or coming. This will be handed to you by Mr. Wilson, a friend of mine, who is by profession an attorney-at-law, and intends to settle in your neighbourhood. You will greatly oblige me by throwing any business in his way you conveniently can. I think you will find him an active man in his profession.

There have been many ups and downs in this neighbourhood since you left. You will no doubt have heard that Charles Nixon was thrown out of Wall-Bottle Colliery by his partners some years ago. He has little to depend on now but the profits of the ballast-machine at Wellington Quay which I dare say are very small. Many of his family have turned out very badly; he has been very unfortunate in family affairs.

If I should have the pleasure of seeing you, I shall give you a long list of occurrences since you and I worked together at Newburn. Hawthorn is still at Wall-Bottle. I dare say you will remember he was a great enemy to me but much more so after you left. I left Wall-Bottle Colliery soon after you and have been very prosperous in my concerns ever since. I am now far above Hawthorn's reach. I am now concerned as civil engineer in different parts of the kingdom. I have only one son whom I have brought up in my own profession. He is now nearly twenty years of age. I have had him educated in the first schools, and he is now at college in Edinbro'. I have found a great want of education myself, but fortune has made me amends for that want.

I am, dear Sir, yours truly,
Geo. Stephenson
I hope Mrs. Locke and your family are all well. My best respects to them.

There are several interesting points about the letter. The first, and most obvious, is that it rather tends to make nonsense of the Smiles' story about enmity between the two men. The tone is friendly and Stephenson believes that they are on sufficiently good terms that he can ask a favour on behalf of his friend the lawyer. Thirdly, it gives more than a hint that Stephenson's life has been transformed since they last met – as indeed it had been. And it was not only his individual status that had changed: the world of the north-eastern collieries was also being dramatically transformed.

The experiments that had begun just before Joseph Locke's birth in developing steam locomotives to run on rails had been abandoned, not because of any failure in the engines themselves, but mainly because the heavy machines fractured brittle, cast-iron rails. There matters might have remained for some time had it not been for the Napoleonic Wars, which caused a huge increase in the price of fodder. The owners of Middleton Colliery, just outside Leeds, relied on horses to haul their coal along a typical railed tramway to be loaded onto boats on the Aire & Calder Navigation. Replacing horses by steam locomotives had obvious advantages if only the problem of broken rails could be solved. Simply building a lighter locomotive was not an option as it would have lacked the necessary power, so a different answer had to be found and what they came up with was a rack and pinion railway. A toothed rail was laid along one side of the tracks, which engaged with cogs on the engine. The extra traction made all the difference and the first locomotives, designed by Matthew Murray and John Blenkinsop, went into operation in 1812, making the Middleton Colliery Railway the world's first successful commercial railway.

Inevitably it attracted a great deal of interest, especially among mine owners in Durham and Northumberland, where many collieries relied on similar tramway systems. That year George Stephenson had just been promoted to a new and important position as engine-wright at Killingworth Colliery and was also placed in charge of all the machines for the Grand Allies, one of the most important colliery groups in the country. As the Chief Engineer he was sent down to see what was happening at Middleton. He duly noted various aspects of the machine developed by Middleton and Murray but did not rush to follow their example.

Other engineers began a series of experiments with locomotives, but without using the rack and pinion system. Among the early successes were locomotives designed by the Chapman brothers and by William Hedley. In 1816, over a year after Hedley's first engine had run on the Wylam tramway that led down to the Tyne, Stephenson joined the fray with his first locomotive, *Blucher,* for the Killingworth tramway. In its main features it was very similar to the Middleton engine, but without the rack and pinion. In some ways it was less advanced than the Hedley engine. In order to raise steam efficiently, the latter had a return flue boiler: the fireman stood at the chimney end of the locomotive, and the flue that carried the gases from the fire was bent into a U-bend, increasing the area in contact with the water in the boiler. Stephenson's engine had a single flue and was constantly having problems raising enough steam to work efficiently.

If this had been Stephenson's only contribution to railway development, his name would have remained no more than a footnote to its history. He was, however, a man of greater vision than many of his contemporaries, and arguably his involvement in the next advance in technology was far more important than anything he achieved in locomotive design. Together with William Losh, partner in the Walker ironworks at Newcastle-upon-Tyne, he developed a vastly improved cast-iron rail, and a new type of chair to hold it in place. The latter did a great deal to overcome the problem of broken rails. Previously, rails had mainly simply met end to end, held in place by the chair with a flat base. This was spiked into a wooden plug in a stone-sleeper block, but if that shifted, the joint became uneven. Stephenson's system had rails meeting in an overlapping joint, and the chair was slightly curved, so that even if the stone settled unevenly, the rails would remain level. It was a major step forward in developing rails that could safely carry heavier locomotives.

Most engineers and mine owners of the day saw locomotive development as little more than a means of replacing horses by machines to continue the work of transporting coal from pithead to navigable waterway. Stephenson had a wider vision: he saw railways as major transport systems to rival roads and waterways. He managed to persuade Edward Pease, a prominent businessman of Stockton-on-Tees, that the line of the proposed Stockton & Darlington Railway should be a public railway, relying mainly on steam locomotives. Impressed by his enthusiastic advocacy, Pease agreed and Stephenson was appointed to the post of Chief Engineer. This was the position he held when he wrote to William Locke.

The Act for making the S&DR railway had originally been passed in 1821, but this had specified nothing out of the ordinary. It was amended in 1823, and the second Act allowed the Company to build steam engines on or near the line, which were intended for cable haulage on steep sections, and to use steam locomotives. Stephenson was then about to take a momentous decision. Existing engineering firms were showing a marked reluctance to use their resources to manufacture the still rudimentary steam locomotives. Stephenson, together with Pease and other investors, agreed to set up their own manufacturing company in Newcastle, which was given the name Robert Stephenson. The latter gave up his university study for his new responsibility – although he had to borrow the money to pay for his portion of the shares. It was to represent a real turning point in railway history and was no less important in the life of Joseph Locke.

In their meeting following the letter from George Stephenson, the two men must have discussed old times and also the fortunes of their two sons. Robert was studying at Edinburgh University, but was not to enjoy the academic life much longer; he was to go into the busy new world of railway engineering. William Locke may perhaps have felt envious of the younger man who had once been his junior and he would certainly have been aware how much brighter young Stephenson's future looked than that of his own son. There is no record of who first broached the subject, but at the end of that meeting it was agreed that Stephenson would take on Joseph as an apprentice at the Newcastle works for three years. In those days it was customary for the family to have to pay to have a son apprenticed, but not on this occasion. On the other hand, Joseph Locke was to be bound for three years, during which he would receive subsistence but no salary.

Young Locke was to divide his time between work and study. After the stultifying life as a clerk and part-time coalman, the young man must have appreciated that this was the opportunity to make a place for himself in the world. He threw himself into both the factory work and his studies with enthusiasm. We have one account of Joseph from those days, from Thomas Tate who taught him maths:

I first saw Mr. Locke at Newcastle-upon-Tyne, about the year 1823. He was a pupil of Mr. George Stephenson's and was occupied during the working hours of each day on his duties at the locomotive manufactory. He was a very active youth, and fond of athletic exercises, in which he excelled; but the chief part of his leisure was devoted to mathematics, and I was so struck with the energy with which he pursued his studies, his quickness of comprehension and indomitable perseverance and I foretold at that early period that he would take a leading part in the profession for which he was destined.

An anonymous writer, who knew him in those days, noted that 'he worked hard, was a quick, determined student, and an excellent swimmer.'

As an apprentice he would learn by experience rather than by formal lessons, but would also be something of a dogsbody, expected to do anything and everything that was demanded of him. There was, however, an unexpected change at Newcastle. Exactly what happened has never been clear, but Robert Stephenson seems to have had some sort of quarrel with his father as a result of which, in 1824, he set sail for South America to work as engineer for a mining company in Mexico. In one sense, it was a loss to Joseph who had become very friendly with Robert, but it also presented him with an opportunity. Alfred Austin, in his autobiography, mentions a manuscript of a memoir written by Joseph but never completed. In the manuscript as described by Austin, Joseph had written that the absence of Robert 'helped him all the more to acquire an early knowledge of the practical parts of his profession of Civil Engineer.'

This suggests that Joseph was no longer spending all his time in the works, but was now getting the opportunity to get out in the field to learn the rudiments of surveying. According to Austin, it was at about this time that Joseph was taken on as an official assistant to George Stephenson 'at a salary then deemed exceptionally handsome'. In fact, although he was now an assistant, it is clear from the official document of agreement dated 11 June 1825 that he was still a trainee:

*George Stephenson undertakes to employ the said Joseph Locke for
two years from the date hereof agrees to pay him an annual salary
of eighty pounds in sterling and also to teach and instruct him in
the Business of an Engineer as now practised by the said George
Stephenson.*

Nevertheless, we do know that in 1825, while still a trainee and still
under 20 years old, he was given the task of overseeing the construction
of a tramway from Black Fell Colliery to the Tyne. It was part of what
was originally an 11½ mile route serving the Grand Allies collieries, but
this section was just 5½ miles. Nevertheless, it was not a straightforward
line, as it required three rope-worked inclines to overcome changes in
level. In these trucks were hauled up and down the slopes by stationary
steam engines. The line had originally been laid out by John Buddle, a
highly successful mining engineer, but the scheme had later been revised
by Stephenson, who was responsible for the overall planning of the
route. Joseph's job would have been that of the Resident Engineer,
taking responsibility for the day-to-day building work. It was a great
responsibility for such a young man, but Stephenson could not really
take care of things himself. He was more than fully occupied making
the final arrangements for the opening of the Stockton & Darlington.
The Black Fell line was eventually to be part of the Bowes Railway and
the inclines remained in use well into the second half of the twentieth
century, and part of the system has been preserved as a unique, surviving
example of this type of early railway operation. The line was intended
for use by locomotives, but when it opened in January 1825 it was
worked by horses. It was to be another year before the first locomotive
had been delivered. Locke, meanwhile, with his colliery line completed,
had to be found other work. It seems it was not always forthcoming.
George Stephenson wrote to Newcastle on 2 March 1826 complaining
about the situation, but at the same time indicating the high regard with
which he now had for the young man:

*Thompson has behaved very badly to Joseph – he said he had no
work for him as soon as he got plenty of water – I had him 3 weeks
at Chester Engines assisting Robert in making the joints – I have
him now at Walker making soda for Mr. Losh ... he is also very
attentive at school and gets forward very well – he is now a very*

good arithmetician and is at present learning Mensuration at which
he makes good progress.

Losh was William Losh of the Walker ironworks in Newcastle, with
whom Stephenson had developed the new, improved type of rail.

While Joseph had been kept busy with his short colliery line, the
Stockton & Darlington was nearing completion. It was officially opened
on 27 September 1825 and thousands turned out for the occasion. It was
obviously an important event, but in its essentials it was still a colliery
line, if on a grander scale than any other. The main business was
conveying coal. Rails were still mounted on stone-sleeper blocks as,
although it was intended for use by locomotives, passengers travelled
in a special coach with flanged wheels, hauled by horses. The rows of
blocks allowed the space between to be kept free for their hooves. There
is no evidence that Stephenson thought very carefully about the gauge,
the distance between the rails, but simply built the line to the same
dimensions as his earlier colliery lines with which he was familiar. This
resulted in a gauge of 4ft 8½ inches. Was this the ideal gauge for a
railway run by locomotives? Whether it was or not, it was destined to
become the standard gauge for Britain's rail network, and it remains so
to this day.

Major civil engineering works were avoided to a large extent by the
use of inclines, along which traffic was moved by stationary steam
engines and cable haulage, to cope with hilly country, as on the Bowes
Railway. The earliest locomotives were still comparatively slow and
cumbersome and not especially reliable. Things were about to change,
for George Stephenson was already involved in a new and far more
ambitious project that was to revolutionise the world of railways and
was to prove a turning point in the career of Joseph Locke.

Chapter Three
THE LIVERPOOL AND MANCHESTER RAILWAY

While Stephenson was busy with the Stockton & Darlington, and Joseph was occupied with his colliery line, a far greater scheme was being proposed across the country in Lancashire: a railway to join the rapidly developing port of Liverpool to Manchester, the commercial heart of the cotton industry. Stephenson was, however, involved from the start. The man behind the proposal was William James of Henley-in-Arden in Warwickshire who had inherited a considerable fortune and established himself as a successful land agent. He was an early enthusiast for railways and, after a meeting with Stephenson, promised to help promote the sale of Killingworth-type locomotives. He visited Liverpool in 1822 and saw that there was an ideal opportunity to promote a line to Manchester. He gained the financial support of a local businessman, James Sanders, who in turn recruited two prominent politicians to the cause, George Canning and William Huskisson. James now set about surveying the possible line. He met with fierce opposition from many local landowners, particularly those with shares in the local canals and also came across a very real physical obstacle that lay across the path of the proposed route, Chat Moss. This was a boggy morass of black, oozy soil that could scarcely support a man's weight.

James persuaded Stephenson to allow his son Robert to join him in the survey team and they seem to have had a good relationship. But things did not go well. James' enthusiasm for the railway led him to neglect his other interests and he was declared bankrupt. The Liverpool & Manchester committee wrote to him in 1824 to tell him that he was no longer needed and that George Stephenson had been invited to take on the job of Chief Engineer. The letter ended somewhat ingenuously: 'I am quite sure that the appointment of Stephenson will under all circumstances be agreeable to you.' It seems more than likely that it was very disagreeable. L.T.C. Rolt in his biography of George and Robert Stephenson suggests that this may have been the event that led to the quarrel between father and son, and that Robert was aggrieved, feeling his father had taken advantage of an old friend. Nevertheless, George Stephenson was now the man in charge.

The problems of surveying had not gone away and Stephenson was now a very busy man indeed, with commitments to railway companies across the country. When Robert left for South America he came to rely more and more on Joseph Locke to act as his assistant. These commitments made it impossible for Stephenson to give the Liverpool & Manchester his full attention and he had to rely on others to carry out much of the survey work unsupervised. When Parliament came to consider the Bill in 1825, the opposition mounted a fierce assault on the engineer, led by their attorney, Alderson. Stephenson later reported: 'I was not long in the witness box before I began to wish for a hole to creep out to.' As the cross examination proceeded it became increasingly clear that the engineer had not examined the work carefully: he did not know exactly where the base line had been set on which the levels were based, nor had he checked the levels himself – and had reluctantly to admit that they might be inaccurate. He had estimated the cost of a bridge over the Irwell without even being able to say how many arches it would contain. And so it went on. In his summing up, Alderson referred to the plan as 'this most absurd scheme' but reserved his most stinging criticism for Stephenson: 'I say he never had a plan – I believe he never had one – I do not believe he is capable of making one' and he ended, 'he is either ignorant or something else which I will not mention.'

The Bill was lost and George Stephenson's reputation had suffered a severe blow. While all this was going on, Joseph Locke was kept busy on the other railway projects. He found time, while back in Newcastle, to write to his friend Robert Stephenson after the disastrous court case on 24 November 1825. It appears that while the father was having a miserable time in England, his son was not much happier in Mexico. Joseph tried to cheer him up and lift 'the melancholy' that had settled over him. Surely, he said, in 'the extent of country which you must see, there must be some objects to create pleasure.' He obviously felt that this was not perhaps as helpful as it might have been in lessening Robert's gloom. 'I might have given further scope to my rallying imagination, and in the most brilliant colours, painted to you my present feelings. But alas I am unqualified with such godlike gifts.' He then went on to describe his own recent experiences:

Since writing to you I have been busily engaged levelling and surveying a proposed line of Railway from Leeds to Hull a distance of 50 miles. This plan is now finished and our directors have fixed not to apply to Parliament until the next sessions but one; about 38 miles is nearly a perfect level and the remaining 12 will require 3 permanent Engines. I have been 8 or 9 months engaged in this survey and have spent my time very comfortably. Amid all the gay scenes which my Wildness led me into I still remember'd you, and the happiness I should have felt to have been with you – but however whilst surveying what do you think I did? Only what others have done – fell in love! And (you may be sure) with one of the most enchanting creatures under Heaven, and my only regret is that we have finished surveying in that neighbourhood.

Since finishing that line I have been levelling one between Manchester and Bolton for which we are going to Parliament next sessions, and I trust the levels will be found to be correct. No doubt but you would hear of this inaccuracy of the Manchester & Liverpool levels which has affected the interest of your Father very much: we must endeavour by our future attention to regain that opinion which we have of late lost.

The manufactory here is quite metamorphosed into a place quite beyond your conception.

The opening of the Darlington Railway has made an impression on the Public which has gain'd your father much popularity.

Having been so much from home this year I cannot give you any home news therefore you must excuse me for not giving you any. Your father and I have been examining the country from here to Hexham for the Carlisle Railway. Hoping to hear from you the first opportunity, believe me my Robert, Your ever faithful Friend,

Joseph Locke.

This long letter makes several interesting points. Firstly, it gives an indication of just how busy the young man was at this time and how much responsibility he had been given. Secondly, that he was behaving like many young men given their freedom from supervision and had started chatting up the local girls: the love affair did not last beyond his stay in the district. Thirdly, it gives an indication of the strong ties that were developing between Joseph and the elder Stephenson. Finally, it hints at just how much Stephenson had lost when the Manchester & Liverpool bill had been rejected. For though the committee intended to try again later, they no longer required his services.

The association with the highly prestigious Liverpool & Manchester appeared to be over as far as the Stephenson camp were concerned. New engineers were appointed, the Act was obtained in 1826 and everything seemed in order. Interestingly, although locomotives were specifically mentioned, it was still referred to as a 'Railway or Tramroad'. But the two brothers, George and John Rennie, who had carried out the new survey with the assistance of their own appointee, Charles Vignoles, now started to create difficulties. There needed to be an appointee to take responsibility for construction of the line, and George Stephenson was again suggested by the committee, along with another very distinguished engineer, John Urpeth Rastrick. The Rennies objected to both and it seemed as if the Rennie tail was trying to wag the committee dog and the dog objected. The end result was that the Rennies had to accept the committee's choice. There was to be more shuffling of names, with Josias Jessop, son of the famous canal engineer, briefly brought in as consultant engineer. George Stephenson was to be the working engineer, looking after the everyday running of the works. It was an unlikely compromise and soon Jessop and Stephenson were at loggerheads and, when the Company backed the latter, Jessop resigned, the Rennies withdrew and Stephenson was now the man in sole charge of operations, though he still had the Rennie appointee, Vignoles, as his assistant. That did not last for long. Vignoles had his own version of what went wrong that he set out in a letter of 14 January 1827, starting with not always agreeing with the great man. He then added: 'I also plead guilty to having neglected to court Mr. S's favour by crying down all other engineers, especially those in London.'

Vignoles had certainly hit on a facet of Stephenson's character, his distrust of London experts. Earlier in his career he had entered a competition to design a safety lamp for use in coal mines. The contest was famously won by Sir Humphry Davy and the Davy safety lamp remains in use. But Stephenson also designed a successful lamp, which was widely used, and a petition was raised in the northeast to reward him appropriately. Davy was infuriated, declaring it was impossible that a mere miner could compete with a qualified scientist like himself and that it was all a fraud. This, coupled with his mauling by Alderson in the House of Commons and his disagreement with the two Rennies, all added to his distrust of professional experts and London experts in particular. This was good news for Joseph Locke, for he was just the sort of man of whom the engineer approved. George had worked alongside his father William Locke and Joseph was no academic, having had little more rudimentary education than George himself. He had learned practical skills on the job and shown himself a willing and enthusiastic pupil. He was to be duly rewarded.

While Stephenson was grappling with Parliament and the Liverpool & Manchester committee, Locke was employed as engineer for the Canterbury & Whitstable Railway, known locally for many years as the Crab & Winkle. The idea for the line was once again initiated by William James, but it was George Stephenson who was to be responsible for its planning. Although the two places are only 9 miles apart, the land in between had a rise of 200 feet and the direct route would have involved gradients far beyond the capabilities of locomotives at that time. So instead, there were to be inclines, worked by stationary engines, at either side of the summit, which was to be cut through by the 828-yard-long Tyler's Hill tunnel. The Act, passed in June 1825, also described it as a 'Railway or Tramroad', with rather more justification than in the case of the Liverpool & Manchester, and Stephenson had even originally suggested that it would be more sensible to work it using horses. But the committee wanted a steam locomotive and an engine *Invicta* was eventually supplied by the Stephenson works.

The initial costs were estimated at £29,400 by another of Stephenson's assistants, John Dixon. Once the Act had been approved, Joseph moved down to take charge. It was scarcely a complex line, single track and running from Whitstable harbour for a little over 6 miles to a village outside Canterbury. Nevertheless, the money ran out before work was completed, largely because tunnelling proved far more expensive than expected. It may have been this experience that began Locke's dislike of tunnels in general, and he tried to avoid them as much as possible. Tunnelling may have been new as far as railway engineers were concerned, but the techniques had been developed over more than half a century of canal building in Britain, culminating in such immense works as the 5415-yard-long Standedge tunnel on the Huddersfield Canal. The railway tunnel was comparatively shallow, just 65 feet below the surface, so should have presented few technical problems. Joseph must, however, have been highly gratified, when in March 1827, the local paper, the *Kent Herald,* praised the accuracy of the engineer's calculations, finding the bores driven from each end met in the middle, the alignment being only out by one inch. Congratulations were a little premature: just a month later part of the roof collapsed and one man was literally carted off to hospital 'covered in blood'. Joseph did not stay for the completion of the work in 1830, called away to more urgent work, but he had the satisfaction of knowing that he had been the engineer for a railway that would have the honour of being the first public railway to run a passenger service with a steam locomotive in April 1830.

Both Dixon and Joseph Locke were required to act as engineers on the Liverpool & Manchester, which was by far the largest enterprise attempted so far in railway construction. The engineering challenges were immense. At the Liverpool end, there were eventually to be three tunnels under the city and the 70-foot deep cutting at Olive Mount that would have to be carved and blasted out of solid sandstone. There was to be an immense viaduct over the Sankey Navigation and a somewhat more modest one across the Bridgewater Canal. Both these waterways had led the fight against the railway and now they would have to endure the humiliating prospect of seeing the railway soaring high above them. There were large embankments to be built including one over a mile long across the valley of the Dilton Brook and a 2-mile-long cutting near Newton-le-Willows. There were to be 63 bridges across the line, one of which at Rainhill carried a road that had to cross the lines at an angle, not at 90°. It was said that building such a bridge caused Stephenson a lot of trouble, and he only solved how to do it by experiments: in this case by carving up a turnip. It hardly seems likely as skew bridges had already been built across several canals, and the engineer needed to go no further than the nearby Lancaster Canal to see examples. The story does, however, show that railway construction was in its infancy and that engineers such as Stephenson were largely self-taught with no formal training.

The actual construction of the line was to be entrusted to four assistants, Joseph Locke, John Dixon and William Allcard, with Daniel Gooch as chief clerk. At the ends of his unpaid apprenticeship, Locke had been offered and accepted a post as Stephenson's assistant at an increased salary of £100 per annum. Now he was employed directly by the Liverpool & Manchester Company at an altogether more handsome rate of £400, equivalent to around £30,000 at today's prices. It was a big step forward both in terms of his personal responsibilities and fortune.

Civil engineering offered many challenges, and no one had yet come up with a solution of how to build a line across Chat Moss. But that was not the only unresolved question. There was a serious disagreement over how the railway was to be run. The Stephenson faction had no doubts: the answer lay with steam locomotives. Others favoured a system of cable haulage, in which carriages and trucks would be pulled along between a series of stationary steam engines. It might seem that this was a question that answered itself, but at that time the only locomotives at work were slow, lumbering and generally unreliable to a greater or lesser degree. The railway committee decided to call in two independent experts to examine the alternatives. The men chosen for the job were both distinguished engineers: James Walker had established his reputation in the first place by building lighthouses, while John Urpeth Rastrick was among the select few with experience of railways. The two investigated existing lines and based their decision largely on the economics of the two systems. They concluded that though it would cost more to build and erect stationary engines than it would to supply locomotives, the running costs of the latter would be far higher. They came down, with no great show of enthusiasm, on the side of the cable-haulage system.

Robert Stephenson was recently returned from South America, and he wrote in disgust to Timothy Hackworth, the engineer now responsible for running the Stockton & Darlington, who had also begun manufacturing and designing locomotives:

They have increased the performance of fixed engines beyond what practice will bear, and, I regret to say, that they have deprecated the locomotive engines below what experience has taught us. I will not say whether these results have arisen from prejudice, or want of information or practice in the subject.

The Stephenson camp decided that they needed to produce a report of their own and the task was entrusted to Joseph Locke and Robert Stephenson. The report, *Observations on the Comparative Merits of Locomotives and Fixed Engines,* set out to refute the arguments in the Walker report. Necessarily much of it is taken up with a detailed examination of costs, since that was the basis of the Walker Rastrick recommendation. It is a lengthy report, but right in the middle is what would seem to be the crucial argument, a review of the problems of working with fixed engines:

> *Who can look upon 30 miles of Railways, divided into equal stages, with 40 trains of carriages, running at the rate of 12 miles an hour, drawn by 20 different steam engines (a delay in any one of which would stop the whole), without feeling that the liability to derangement alone is sufficient to render the stoppages extremely uncertain? And in considering this long chain of connected power, with the continual crossings of the trains from one line to the other and subject to the government of no fewer than 150 men, whose individual attention is required to preserve the communication between two of the most important towns in the kingdom. We cannot but express our decided conviction that a system which necessarily involves by a single accident, the stoppage of the whole, is totally unsuited to a Public Railway.*

It was a well thought-out and well-written document, but it had an unfortunate and unexpected side effect. The two young engineers had done all the work but as it was being got ready for publication, George Stephenson suddenly demanded that it should be put out under his name on the grounds that it was all based on his findings. Robert would have been happy to go along with this, but Locke felt the injustice of the request. He was, it seems, rather more of his father's man than had first appeared and he stuck firmly to the position that he and Robert must be named as authors. Eventually a compromise was reached and the title page contained the wording 'Compiled from the reports of George Stephenson.' The matter had been resolved, but it was the first time that Locke had refused to agree with his old master.

In the event neither side won the argument over which system should be adopted. There remained a feeling that even though the locomotive might be a better alternative, there was still a lingering suspicion that the machine was not yet ready to run a successful railway over such a distance. It was decided to put the matter to the test. Henry Booth, the Company Secretary, put an advert in several newspapers: 'The Directors of the Liverpool and Manchester Railway hereby offer a Premium of £500 (over and above the cost price) for a Locomotive Engine, which shall be a decided improvement on any hitherto constructed.'

The rules specified the requirements the entrants had to meet. Weight must not exceed six tons if on six wheels and four and a half tons on four wheels, while boiler pressure was limited to 50 pounds per square inch. A six-wheeled engine had to be capable of hauling a train of carriages, together with the tender of 20 tons at 10 miles per hour: smaller engines having proportionally smaller loads.

Robert Stephenson was now in charge of preparing what was initially known simply as 'the premium engine', and it was decided to go for the smaller, four-wheeled version. By the time the closing date for entry into the competition arrived there were five contestants. One, built in Scotland, never made it to the test site and another could scarcely be said to meet the requirements of the competition. It was worked by a horse on a treadmill. The other two were serious competitors. Timothy Hackworth from the Stockton & Darlington built his contender, *Sans Pareil* at his Soho works at Shildon, Durham. It was a sound, sturdy machine, based very much on existing locomotives, with a return flue boiler, a pair of vertical cylinders and two pairs of coupled drive wheels. A replica of this and the other contesting engines was built for the 150th anniversary of the event and I was fortunate enough to be present when *Sans Pareil* was first fired up. It was an impressive and powerful engine, but it represented no form of new thinking.

The same could not be said of the next entrant, *Novelty*, designed by the team of John Braithwaite and John Ericsson, based not on early locomotives but on Braithwaite's design for a fire engine. It was very lightweight, with a vertical boiler and two cylinders driving down through a bell crank to a cranked axle; water for the boiler was held in a tank below the platform. It certainly lived up to its name and was the pre-contest favourite. It looked fast and sporty, but George Stephenson took one look and summed it up very differently: no guts.

The premium engine itself soon developed some wholly new features. The most important was suggested to Robert by the railway Company Secretary Henry Booth, who had correctly identified the major fault of earlier locomotives as poor steaming. He suggested that instead of just a return flue in the boiler, there should be a large number of tubes that would carry the hot gases from the firebox that would itself be enclosed by a water jacket. To ensure there was sufficient heat from the fire, the exhaust steam, instead of being simply released into the atmosphere, would be turned up the chimney. This would draw more air through the firebox, increasing the temperature. This device of blast-pipe exhaust was not new: Trevithick had used it many years before. This raises an intriguing possibility.

After his failure to interest anyone in his steam locomotives, Trevithick had accepted an offer to set up his high-pressure engines at a silver mine in Peru. He sent over the machinery and a working party, but when they had difficulties he resolved to go and sort things out himself. He left England in 1816. It was originally intended to be a short visit, but due to a number of different circumstances, including the appropriation of the mine and of the engineer's promised payment of bullion, by Simon Bolivar's army, he was to stay for years not months. After many adventures, the engineer had finally arrived at Cartagena in 1827, hoping to make his way home. He had been mining gold in Mexico and, in the hope of finding a route for his bullion to the coast, he had set off on foot and had suffered a series of mishaps and accidents, so that he had arrived virtually penniless. Robert Stephenson also came to Cartagena from his mining experience in South America and the two met. Robert loaned the older engineer the money to pay his fare home. The two must have talked about what had happened in the world of railways and it is tempting to think that Trevithick mentioned his own experiments with exhaust blast.

The third novel feature of the premium engine was the setting of the cylinders, no longer vertical but sloping at an angle of 45°. They supplied the drive via a connecting rod to the front wheels. Once it was completed it was given a name, *Rocket*. The actual trial was held on the line at Rainhill in October 1829. The locomotives were required to make runs with their loads up and down a length of track, equivalent to the return journey between Liverpool and Manchester. The crowd's favourite was still *Novelty*, which looked slick and speedy, but Stephenson's early judgement proved accurate. It was never able to complete the course. Interestingly, the replica of this engine proved equally unreliable. *Sans Pareil* suffered from a series of technical problems and had to be withdrawn. The Hackworth camp always claimed that the fault was all due to a cracked cylinder that had been cast at the Stephenson Works in Newcastle. There were dark mutterings of espionage but even if the locomotive had completed the course, it would have been unlikely to match *Rocket*'s performance. That engine sailed through the trials and on the final day achieved not just the ten miles an hour stipulated in the rules but an unprecedented thirty. It was just as well that this was the locomotive that won, for with its new features it represented the way forward. Future steam locomotives would be developed from this prototype. Robert Stephenson himself would at once begin developing locomotives designed not just to pass the requirements of a trial but to run a main-line service. They would evolve to become the efficient Planet Class. Meanwhile work was proceeding on building the line.

Locke must have been delighted with his new responsible position in this great undertaking, which involved him working on many different parts of the line. He was involved in the construction of the immense Broad Green embankment, which, on his own calculations, involved the removal of 600,000 cubic yards of material. There were other major obstacles to be overcome, not least the crossing of Chat Moss. He was initially put in charge of the work on this part of the line. A start was made by digging drainage ditches, but as fast as they were dug, the black, slimy mud oozed back in again. Working on the site was difficult, local farmers crossed the Moss by fastening planks to their feet to spread the load. However, before the work could be completed, Locke was sent to look after the work at the Liverpool end. John Dixon, another trusted Stephenson man, was brought down from Darlington. He did not make the ideal start. Plank walkways were laid, Dixon slipped off early in his period on site and began disappearing into the bog and had to be hauled out by the navvies. Stephenson noted that the tough, coarse plants that spread over the surface of the morass seemed like miniature rafts. He reasoned that if he did build a raft, eventually an equilibrium point would be reached, when it would be stable. He piled on brushwood and heather and loaded his rafts with spoil, but the material kept on sinking out of sight. As Stephenson himself noted, even Locke and Dixon began to doubt the scheme would work. But eventually the bank remained above the surface and by New Year's Day 1830 a single track could be laid and Chat Moss had been conquered.

Meanwhile, there were troubles with tunnelling at the Liverpool end. There were to be two tunnels from Edgehill: one to the docks, the Wapping tunnel, and the other to Crown Street station: it was the former that had been surveyed by Charles Vignoles. The first shaft was sunk in September 1826 and, two months later, Stephenson informed the directors that there was a serious misalignment in the headings and found it convenient to blame Vignoles. Stephenson was perhaps fortunate, in that in his earlier dealings, when assistants had been found to make serious errors, he as the Chief Engineer had been forced to shoulder the blame. This time he achieved exactly what he wanted: Vignoles went and Joseph Locke took charge. In later evidence to the Brighton line Parliamentary Committee, he gave details of the tunnelling. The tunnel was a mile and a quarter long, 16ft high and 22ft wide, driven through a mixture of sandstone, blue shale, rock clay and newly formed earth. Locke wrote to Robert Stephenson on 28 February 1827, reporting on progress and telling him that his father's reputation was held in high esteem:

> On the Tunnel we are going very well, and I hope very correctly – at least I spare neither pains in watching every part of it. I assure you I have had a busy time of it since I came here – and that present prospect is even more busy…I have strove to assist and advance the interest of your father which in return has advanced mine and has ever placed that confidence in me of which I am proud…I know not how the manufacture goes on at Newcastle, I fear not so briskly as has done – I believe Mr. Longbridge wishes to decline the Engine business until your return. Thos Nicholson has left and is now at college in Edinburgh???… I understand the Darlington railway is doing very well, and gives great satisfaction; they are just contracted for another Locomotive Engine. I have recently been joined in my labours by your friend J. Dixon, who has taken the Manchester end of the line.

Things were indeed going well with Locke and he must have felt settled in to his very prestigious work as Resident Engineer for the Liverpool end of the railway, but a disagreement broke out between the railway committee and Stephenson. The engineer had more than one project on the go and regarded Joseph as his personal assistant who could be sent to wherever he was needed. The committee, not unreasonably, felt that as they were paying a handsome salary to the young man they should have exclusive use of his services. Things came to a head when Stephenson directed Locke to go and attend to matters on the line under construction between Manchester and Stockport. Stephenson insisted that Locke's presence on that line was crucial and that the interests of the Liverpool & Manchester would not suffer in his absence. The directors disagreed, and neither side was prepared to compromise. It left Locke in a most uncomfortable position. He had huge respect for George Stephenson who had been his mentor, as the letter quoted above makes clear, and had no wish to antagonise him. On the other hand, the job of assistant on the Liverpool & Manchester was both well paid and highly prestigious. In the event, he felt he had only one option: he resigned and left for the Stockport line. There really was no choice: he could hardly have opted to stay on and opposed Stephenson, who was not a man to take disloyalty lightly. It was not, however, to be the end of his involvement with the line.

After he had left the Liverpool & Manchester, he was called back by the directors and asked to look at the other tunnel under construction to what would eventually become the main Liverpool passenger station at Lime Street. There had been alarming reports of inaccuracies. Locke was forced to report that there were, indeed, serious inaccuracies. According to his biographer Joseph Devey, 'several portions of the tunnel would never have formed a straight line; and, in one instance, two parts of the tunnel, instead of meeting, would have given each other the go-by altogether.' He showed his report first to his successor, overlooking the works, who agreed it was a fair assessment, and it was duly passed on to the Board. Devey excused the errors, on the grounds that 'the accurate use of delicate instruments, such as spirit-levels, theodolites, and miners' compasses, is not intuitively understood by any, and only mastered by a few.' The argument hardly stands up to scrutiny, given the huge advances made over the previous half-century or more on constructing canal tunnels. There is no doubt that the report would have been a huge embarrassment to Stephenson, while writing it and, in effect, criticising work for which his old mentor was responsible, must have been no less uncomfortable for Locke. Fortunately it was possible to rectify the mistakes in the tunnel survey and the line moved steadily towards completion. One of the men engaged in constructing the tunnel was the contractor William Mackenzie. Railway work was as new to him as to most engineers and contractors at that time, but he showed remarkable enthusiasm for the job. His enthusiasm was not always shared by an unwilling companion, the young engineer David Stevenson:

> *I have spent many a weary hour and I might say night, because Mackenzie ... would often, after finishing his pipe and glass of brandy and water ... go out to one of the shafts which, as ill luck would have it, was close to his house and if, by further bad luck he found a bucket going down he would at once cry, 'Now then Stevenson, let us jump in and see what these fellows are about down below.'...and the whole night's expedition terminated in making our exit into daylight at 4 or 5 in the morning.*

Mackenzie was to play an important role in Locke's career, as we shall see later.

The date fixed for a ceremonial opening of the line was Wednesday, 15 September 1830. By now a number of new, improved versions of *Rocket* had been built at the Stephenson works in Newcastle. They were no longer limited by the size and other restrictions imposed for the competition with one notable exception: they were still required to 'consume their own smoke'. In practice, this meant using coke instead of coal for firing. In all there were to be eight trains of carriages, hauled by locomotives in this order: *Northumbrian, Phoenix, North Star, Rocket, Dart, Comet, Arrow* and *Meteor*. Although he was no longer employed by the Company, Joseph Locke was given the honour of driving *Rocket*, an honour which, in view of later events, he must have often wished had gone to someone else. The Orders of the Day laid out what was to happen:

> *When the Trains of Carriages are attached to their respective Engines a Gun will be fired as a preliminary signal, when the* Northumbrian *will take her place at the head of the Procession: a second Gun will then be fired, and the whole will move forward.*
> *The Engines will stop at Parkside (a little beyond Newton) to take*

in a supply of water, during which the company are requested not to leave their Carriages.

Everything, it seemed, had been catered for, including the safety of the expected crowds of onlookers. Railings had been set up along the edge of Olive Mount cutting to prevent anyone toppling over the edge.

The occasion attracted huge crowds, as reported in the Liverpool paper *The Albion*:

All the hotels, inns, and taverns in the town and its vicinity were crowded to excess. A number of private houses were also filled with strangers. So that there was, on Wednesday morning, a greater concourse of strangers in Liverpool than there had ever been before at one time in its annals.

The guest of honour was the Duke of Wellington, not perhaps the happiest choice, since he was very far from being a railway enthusiast. And though to many of the nation he was the Hero of Waterloo, in the northwest, and in Manchester in particular, he was the Villain of Peterloo. It was his political party that had ordered in the cavalry to break up a peaceful meeting in Manchester to call for parliamentary reform, an action that resulted in many deaths and injuries. Nevertheless, he was treated with great dignity and was to travel the line in a specially prepared eight-wheeled carriage, handsomely decorated with gilded moulding and covered with a crimson canopy: 'the whole had a magnificent and imposing effect, in the Grecian style of architecture.'

All went well at first and *Northumbrian* made its scheduled stop at Parkside, and was shunted off the main running track. Several of the passengers now got out and began to roam all over the lines, ignoring the regulations. It was not perhaps surprising: few, if any, of those present were familiar with railways, and those who had a knowledge would only have seen the older, slow colliery engines. They did not appreciate the speeds now attainable and the danger the new locomotives represented.

William Huskisson MP was of a very different political persuasion from the Duke, as radical as the latter was conservative, and there was a history of personal antagonism between the two men. However, the Duke leaned out of his carriage and seemed to be offering a conciliatory handshake: Huskisson moved across to join him. Then there were shouts that a locomotive was on its way. *Rocket* was approaching at speed and people began to scramble hastily back into their coaches. Huskisson, who had been ill recently, seemed confused. He clung to the door of the Duke's carriage. *Rocket* hit the door, flinging Huskisson onto the tracks, where he was run over and his thigh crushed.

A Birmingham man, Joseph Parkes, lifted him from the rails.

'This is the death of me,' murmured Huskisson.

'I hope not sir,' said Parkes.

'Yes it is.'

Every effort was made to help the injured man. *Northumbrian* was detached from its train and a flat car that had held a band of musicians was coupled up. Huskisson was laid carefully on top, and the locomotive sped away with George Stephenson taking control. The locomotive reached 36mph, but speed could not save Huskisson, and the man who had done so much to promote railways died.

One can only imagine Joseph Locke's feelings on that day, as triumph became tragedy. There was no question of blame attached to him: there was nothing he could have done to prevent the accident, which was caused by disregard of the rules for the day. There were attendants in charge of each train, but they would hardly have dared tell such important guests what to do. When such accidents happen today, the unfortunate driver would be given counselling and support, but no such services existed then. He had to cope with the fact that he had killed a man and get on with his life.

Meanwhile, the organisers had to decide what to do. The crowds were gathered at Manchester so it was decided to go ahead with the programme as originally planned. The Duke had left Liverpool to the cheers of the crowd: he arrived at Manchester to boos and brickbats. He appeared calm and must have expected a rowdy reception, and the return journey passed relatively uneventfully. Due to the detachment of *Northumbrian* everything had got out of order and darkness was falling by the time they got back to Liverpool. There was, however, the dramatic finish of a journey down the Edgehill tunnel, lit by gas lamps.

Though marred by tragedy, the day had proved that there was a huge interest in and enthusiasm for railways, and the following day when the line was opened to the general public, there was a clamour for tickets. The Liverpool & Manchester Railway was not only built on a larger scale than its predecessors, but it had vividly demonstrated that passenger travel would in the future prove as important as the movement of freight. For Joseph Locke it had provided an opportunity to learn a range of different skills and prove himself to be a trustworthy and highly competent engineer.

Chapter Four
THE GRAND JUNCTION

With the successful opening of the Liverpool & Manchester and the triumph of the steam locomotive over cable haulage, the expansion of the rail system was inevitable. Plans were soon being made to join the line to Birmingham and to build on from there with a line to London. For both Joseph Locke and Robert Stephenson it was a time of great opportunity, and both were eager to grab their chances. Robert was soon to be appointed as the Chief Engineer for the new London & Birmingham Railway, but Joseph's path to success was to prove altogether more tortuous. He was, however, ready to accept any challenge. He had served his apprenticeship as an assistant engineer and proved his abilities in civil engineering. He had learned how things should be done and, just as importantly, had developed a pretty good idea of how they should not be done. Both lessons had been learned from George Stephenson.

Locke had seen the problems that had arisen when Stephenson had failed to take full control of operations. They had been apparent early on in the construction of the Liverpool & Manchester, when the great engineer had entrusted vital work to often inexperienced assistants and an ill-organised workforce. Thomas Telford had been asked to report on the state of the workings at the end of November 1828. He would have expected to find such a major undertaking parcelled out between experienced contractors, who would have been given precise instructions and specifications. He sent one of his best men, James Mills, to find out exactly what was being done. His report of 7 December was not what Telford had expected to receive:

There is some difficulty in making out correctly the value of what is to do, for in truth there does nor appear to be a single contract existing on the whole line. Stevenson [sic] seems to be the contractor for the whole, and to employ all the different people at such prices as he thinks proper to give them, the company finding all Materials, not only rails and wagons, but even Wheelbarrows and Planks &c.

Telford was horrified and wrote a scathing comment of his own, but nothing much changed. Joseph Locke would not make the same mistake. The different approaches to construction were to set the young man and his mentor in a destructive opposition that would sour their relationship forever. At this stage, however, things were going reasonably smoothly. Locke had gone to Ireland with Stephenson to look over the proposed line from Dublin to Kingston in February 1832, which when it opened in 1834 was to be that country's first railway. Inevitably, with Stephenson's involvement in the project, it was built to his 4ft 8½in gauge, but unlike the lines in the rest of the British Isles it was not to become the standard. Later routes were built to 5ft 3in and the Dublin & Kingston was eventually converted to the new Irish standard in 1857.

Back in England plans were beginning to be laid for the connections between the Liverpool & Manchester and Birmingham. There was already a short spur off the former route, the Warrington & Newton Railway, and the directors of that Company were understandably anxious that their line should be included in the through route, which became known as the Grand Junction Railway. George Stephenson was very much the man of the moment and he was called in to advise on the likeliest route, but it was Robert who carried out the survey. He proposed a route through Sandbach. The route was opposed by the Marquess of Stafford, who was also the 1st Duke of Sutherland, the man mainly known for instigating the infamous Highland Clearances. He had been among the earliest promoters of canals in his younger days and had a considerable income from the Bridgewater Canal. He had, however, been quick to see the potential in rail travel and had acquired a 20 per cent share in the Liverpool & Manchester. It is not known exactly why he opposed the Sandbach route, but as it was the Liverpool men who were promoting the line, his voice could not be ignored. As a result, Joseph Locke was sent off to survey an alternative route. It was still connected to the Warrington & Newton, but took a different line, past Crewe Hall and the tiny hamlet of Crewe, that was destined to become famous in railway history.

Not everyone was happy with the proposed route, and Charles Vignoles was given the task of finding a more direct alternative. His route involved the construction of a massive – and very costly – viaduct across the Mersey at Runcorn. There was even a proposal for an even more expensive alternative, a tunnel under the river. In the event, costs for the direct routes ruled them out, and it was the Locke line that was accepted. Now all that remained to be done was to reach an agreement with the owners of the Warrington & Newton. At first there was a good deal of quibbling about the price that would be paid for shares. The Grand Junction were aware that the line, just 4¾ miles long, would need considerable upgrading, and needed to set the price to take that into account. It was only a small part of a route that would have to run for another 77 miles to reach Birmingham, but an important part. When negotiations seemed stuck, Locke was asked to look at alternatives. In the event, he estimated that even paying over £100 a share and paying for the upgrade, with what would be a new, improved track, would still be the better option. The shares were bought for £114 6s each, and everyone declared themselves happy.

The directors of the Grand Junction were more than satisfied with Locke's part in the proceedings to date, but there was never much doubt about who would be asked to take on the post of Chief Engineer. It could only be the now famous George Stephenson. In spite of recent differences, Locke probably felt confident that, having done so much of the preparatory surveying, he would be appointed Resident Engineer to take charge of the day-to-day construction work. When the Bill was passed, Stephenson began to make his arrangements: he wanted to follow the system he had used on the Liverpool & Manchester, with the line divided into three and Joseph being simply an assistant on part of the route. The directors were unhappy with the suggestion and Locke was even less happy: he knew he had earned better.

Negotiations got nowhere at first, so Locke eventually felt that he had no alternative but to withdraw from the whole enterprise. That was a situation that was even less to the directors' liking; they wanted him to be involved in a major capacity. There was some hurried rethinking. A new proposal was brought forward. Stephenson would be Chief Engineer, but Locke would be Resident Engineer, with responsibility for the northern section – and would take over the whole in Stephenson's absence. According to Devey's biography, the great engineer declared that he would never be absent to give Locke a chance to interfere. If those were his words, or his true feelings, then it would seem that this would be an arrangement that would not last very long. So it was to prove.

The first matter that had to be considered was the letting of contracts. Locke was well aware that this was of the very greatest importance, and set out his ideas to the directors. In his opinion it was the main job of the engineer to provide detailed plans and specifications for the line, so that no one was in any doubt about what the work would entail. Secondly, he felt that as railway construction was so new, contracts should only be let out in ten-mile parcels, to ensure that no contractors were able to take on more work than they could actually perform. George Stephenson preferred to follow the far looser system that he had used on other lines. The judgement of the two men was about to be put to the test.

By the end of September 1834, all the lots laid out by Locke had been tendered for and agreed. The estimates prepared by the engineering staff were in close agreement with those of the contractors and everyone was delighted. By November, the remaining lots for the section under the control of Stephenson and his assistant had still not been settled. What was even worse, there were huge discrepancies between the engineers' and contractors' estimates. Not surprisingly, the Company found this situation alarming, so Locke was asked to do his own checks. It rapidly became apparent that the information supplied by Stephenson was so vague that the contractors were relying largely on guesswork, and upping the price simply to make sure that they covered all eventualities. The most striking example was the Penkridge viaduct for which the contractor had estimated a cost of £26,000. Locke then provided him with an exact specification, setting out clearly and precisely what was required. The contractor now came up with a figure of £6,000, said to include a handsome profit for himself.

The directors could only draw one conclusion, but they were still loath to lose the great engineer and suggested that the two men should act jointly as chief engineers. This arrangement was even less likely to work than the previous one, and in August 1835, Stephenson withdrew and Joseph Locke was now Chief Engineer for the Grand Junction Railway. There was to be an interesting corollary to the story of the Penkridge viaduct, and it starts during the construction of the Sankey viaduct for the Liverpool & Manchester. Stephenson needed to find a source of good stone and he found what he needed in a quarry managed by a young man from Birkenhead, Thomas Brassey. The two must have got on well, for Stephenson suggested to him that he should apply for one of the Grand Junction contracts. He put in a tender for the huge Dutton viaduct, but his offer was £6,000 higher than that of a rival contractor, the far more experienced David McIntosh. He then tried for the ten-mile stretch that would include Penkridge. It was here that he was successful.

According to one story, Locke got up early one morning at his lodgings in Liverpool, breakfasted, walked to the ferry, crossed the Mersey and arrived at Brassey's Birkenhead home at eight in the morning. They discussed the Penkridge contract and reached a rapid agreement. Brassey must have been impressed by Locke's energy and it seems Locke in turn was equally impressed by Brassey's enthusiasm. He and Joseph Locke were the same age, and it was to prove the start of a long and successful collaboration. They not only worked together on many major projects but also became good friends.

Brassey was not the only contractor on the line who was to have a long working relationship with Locke. William Mackenzie was born into a family who had been involved with civil engineering projects since the start of the Canal Age. He was the eldest of the eleven children of Alexander Mackenzie, whose first encounter with these works was as a navvy on the Forth & Clyde Canal, but he soon rose through the ranks and became a contractor on the Leeds & Liverpool Canal. William was born in Lancashire and at first it seemed he might take a different path, as he was apprenticed to a weaver. That life did not suit him and he was soon following in his father's footsteps. Over the years he was to work on many important projects and spent some time with Thomas Telford. One of the biggest schemes he worked on was the construction of a new main line for the Birmingham Canal, a task that involved immense earthworks, including some of the deepest cuttings ever made for a transport route at that time. On this project he was actually appointed as the Resident Engineer. So when the Canal Age gave way to the Railway Age he was ideally suited for the new world, with a wealth of experience behind him. He took a contract on the tunnel between Edge Hill and Lime Street and, whatever fault Locke may have found with the engineers supervising the work, he clearly laid no blame on the contractor, for he was given the very important contract for the Warrington end of the Grand Junction, worth £43,000.

Things did not always go smoothly. It was decided to realign the route near Warrington, which involved moving the site for the viaduct across the Irwell. This inevitably caused delays while negotiations went ahead to purchase the new land needed for the realignment. Mackenzie grumbled in a letter of 19 June 1835 that his bricklayers had been idle for three weeks 'and I need not add that Bricklayers do not relish Idleness in the Month of June.' Apart from this small setback, work went on smoothly to the satisfaction of both contractor and engineer. The two men appear to have respected each other but their relationship was scarcely amicable as will appear later.

We are fortunate in having a detailed description of the line in *The Book of the Grand Junction* by Thomas Roscoe, published in 1839. The title page includes the inscription, directly beneath the author's name 'And the Resident Engineers', so one can be reasonably certain that the technical information is accurate. The book is primarily written to give travellers on the line a detailed account of all the places of interest they will pass along the way, and occasionally throws up surprises. Today, one can hardly imagine Runcorn being described as 'the little town and bathing place.' Various stately homes are described, one of which was the home of James Watt Jnr., son of the famous steam engine pioneer. There is a slight irony in this, as James Watt Snr. had resolutely opposed all attempts to use high-pressure steam. As a result, when his Cornish agent William Murdoch built a model of a steam carriage to go on the roads, he was told peremptorily to give up his endeavours or find another job. He stuck with the job, and now his son could see the chance the family had missed to be at the head of the revolution in steam transport. However, he had a revenge of sorts. In the original Act it was specified that the line could not pass through his estates without his permission. In spite of the best efforts of the Company to come to terms with him he steadfastly refused to co-operate. The Company made the best of it, and the Chairman was able to report with some glee that it had all worked out well when they had looked for a new route, as the chairman, John Moss, wrote in December 1834:

In this they have succeeded beyond their expectations; they have come to terms with nearly the whole of the land-owners between the points of deviation and the Town of Birmingham by which all chance of opposition is removed. The line, though longer than the original one by about a mile, is preferable in all other respects being less expensive and affording better levels besides avoiding a tunnel under the Town.

The main interest, as far as the story of Joseph Locke is concerned, lies not so much with wrangles over land purchase, as with the details of the engineering features along the way.

The first structure of importance to be described was the River Rea viaduct at the Birmingham end of the line. It makes an impressive start, a structure of stone and blue brick, a thousand foot long and carried on twenty-eight arches. Designed by Locke, it was carefully planned as Roscoe explained: 'Each pier is embedded at the foundation in a mass of concrete, consisting of gravel and quick lime of two feet thickness, with a central cast iron pipe and grate through which all the surface water is carried from the road.' No expense was spared and high quality stone was brought from quarries at Long Eaton in Derbyshire. This was followed by a long, curved embankment standing 12-13ft high.

Further along, the River Tame was diverted to make way for the tracks and the great Aston embankment was constructed, containing an estimated 300,000 cubic yards of material. It was to prove one of the most difficult undertakings on the line:

Several accidents occurred in the course of raising the embankment, which had well nigh frustrated all the plans of the Engineer, and effectually prevented its completion by the time determined upon for the opening of the line to the public. The foundation of the embankment which skirted the old course of the river, consisted of deposits left from the time of the stream, to the depth of many feet, which being too weak to maintain its weight, in many instances gave way, and were forced out and, in one case, the embankment sank nearly the depth of eight feet in the course of an hour.

Eventually, the workers managed to get down to firm ground and the great bank was stabilised.

Locke used the technique known as 'cut and fill,' pioneered by the canal engineers, and seen at its most dramatic on the main line of what is now the Shropshire Union Canal. The material excavated in the deep cuttings through rising ground would be used to build embankments across the low valleys. A cutting near Newton was 80ft below the surface at its deepest point, and 200,000 cubic yards were removed. Roscoe gave a rather poetic description of what work on a great cutting involved:

> *By day the bright sunbeams, broken by the numerous angles which each successive advance presented to its linear ray, lay scattered in shining fragments upon the sloping banks, cheering the toil-worn labourers, - by night the hill literally swarmed with moving bodies, lighted to their work like torches flickering from side to side, and from place to place. Creaking cranes, dragging up by ropes and pulleys the laden barrows with their guides, and again slowly securing their descent down the almost perpendicular banks - the clatter of continued footsteps, the heavy sound of spade and pickaxe, and the busy hum of toiling men, completed a scene of unexampled animation.*

What is being described here is a barrow run, work rather dreaded by the navvies. They had to balance the loaded barrows as they were hauled up the steep plank walkways by the cranes, and then run back down with the empties. The planks would be greasy with wet clay and, if a man slipped, the best he could do was throw himself to one side and the barrow to the other to avoid the whole load crashing down on top of him.

The most imposing structures on the whole line were two viaducts, both crossing the Weaver as it inconveniently went through a great loop, right in the path of the line. The first at Vale Royal had five arches, each with a 63ft span and 20ft high, but the second at Dutton was far grander. It had twenty arches and rose 60ft above the river and took 3 years to build at a cost of £60,000. Roscoe described it as 'most extraordinary and magnificent' and the finest to be built 'since the days of the Romans', a difficult claim to justify.

There were other problems to face along the way. At two points the line had to cross an area of peat bog, but these must have seemed minor obstacles to a man who had once been involved in conquering Chat Moss. At the larger of the two bogs he used the same tactic as that employed by Stephenson of laying down brushwood. Another section of the line demonstrated Locke's confidence in the development of the steam locomotive. One obstacle he had to overcome was the hill from Crewe to Madeley with a total rise of nearly 400 feet. This would have seemed an impossible obstacle to the first railway engineers, who would probably have felt it necessary to construct an incline and stationary engine. Joseph decided to meet it head on, even though it involved a stretch of 3 miles at a gradient of 1 in 177. It must have seemed folly to some at the time, but he was to go on to build lines with even stiffer climbs in the future.

Crewe itself had not yet developed, but unlike Watt, Lord Crewe of nearby Crewe Hall welcomed the arrival of the railway. Thanks to his influence Crewe station was first class, even though when built no one had much reason to alight there, and he built a hotel in anticipation of future traffic. The Crewe Arms still exists and has a handsome façade of brick with stone mouldings round windows and doors and topped with a balustrade. Externally it has changed very little, but the interior has been modernised, though it does still contain some original features including a magnificent, carved-marble fireplace. The growth of Crewe as a major junction and railway town will be dealt with in a later chapter.

Rather surprisingly, one of the features that gave the most trouble was an aqueduct that had to be built to carry a short arm of the Birmingham Canal over the tracks. Cast-iron aqueducts had by this date been built on a number of different canals, and the technology was well understood. Yet when water was let in, the structure leaked so badly that it had to be drained, sealed off and almost completely rebuilt. It would have seemed a minor work in the planning stage, yet it was the one thing that delayed the opening, if not for very long.

One aspect of the line that Roscoe did not comment on himself was the track. It was here that Locke proved to be innovative and was to make a major advance. The Liverpool & Manchester had initially been laid with fish-belly rails, so-called because the underside was curved. They were comparatively light at just 35lb per yard, though the weight of rails on the line had to be increased in later years, and were mounted on stone sleeper blocks, following the pattern set on earlier tramways and on the Stockton & Darlington. Locke knew that the stone blocks were easily moved, causing the lines to slip out of gauge. He introduced transverse wooden sleepers and a very different type of rail. This was double-headed, looking in cross section like a dumb-bell. This was keyed into iron chairs using hardwood wedges, with each rail sloping slightly inwards towards the middle of the track. The original idea was that the rails could be reversed as the top became worn, but this never worked in practice. Locke was later to be called in to give evidence to a special committee set up by the London & North Western Railway in 1843 to give evidence on the best way of laying track and the best type of rail. By this date he was recommending rails weighing 85lb per yard. Other techniques and designs would be tried over the years, including longitudinal sleepers used on Brunel's Great Western and flat-bottomed rails, designed by Charles Vignoles, that were to prove very popular in North America. But it was the double-headed rail set on transverse sleepers that became the norm for British railway tracks and the establishment of this system is by no means the least of Locke's engineering achievements.

The Grand Junction opened with a comparatively modest ceremony on 4 July 1837, with two trains, each of three coaches, all named: one leaving from Manchester with *Celerity*, *Umpire* and *Swallow*, the other from Liverpool with *Triumph*, *Greyhound* and *Statesman*. At Newton Junction, the trains were united to be hauled for the rest of the journey by a suitably bedecked locomotive, *Wildfire*. A significant addition to the inaugural train was a pair of mail coaches, one from each city. Mail coaches had first been introduced on the Liverpool & Manchester and offered railway companies a potentially valuable source of revenue. Unfortunately the Grand Junction appears to have made a rather poor deal with the Post Office initially and had to renegotiate it. The opening ceremony passed without incident, which must have been a great relief to Locke after the traumatic experience of the Liverpool & Manchester opening and his all too direct involvement in the death of Huskisson.

The directors must have been delighted to have decided to stay with Locke, even though when the Chairman issued his first report early in 1838, he was careful to include a note of gratitude for the initial work carried out by Stephenson. There is, however, no doubt that they were well aware that it was Joseph Locke's scrupulous care in defining the work and issuing contracts that had resulted in a railway being constructed on time and at the comparatively modest cost of £20,000 per mile – less than half that of the contemporary London & Birmingham, though the latter contained far more taxing engineering challenges and land purchase had been expensive. The first year after the opening was, however, not without its problems.

A bridge collapsed near Warrington, blocking the line and passengers had to leave the train and walk across planks to join a train on the far side of the blockage to finish their journey: not very good for customer relations. Soon after that there was a more serious event. Frost broke up the clay round the short tunnel at Preston Brook leading to a partial collapse and once again temporary measures had to be taken to move passengers from one train to another. These were, however, minor incidents that were quickly dealt with and did nothing to reduce the popularity of the line. To the great satisfaction of the shareholders the line showed immediate profit and paid handsome dividends of never less than 10 per cent. Small wonder that the Chairman in that first report was even more fulsome on the subject of Joseph Locke than he had been on George Stephenson:

> *The execution of the works, with all the variety of detail belonging to it, had devolved wholly upon Mr. Locke, the Engineer in Chief, who has devoted himself to the discharge of his duties, responsible duties, with an ability, zeal, and above all, an untiring energy which have fully justified the implicit confidence which has been reposed on him on all occasions; and it is gratifying to relate that he has earned for himself, in the service of this Company a reputation which will confer upon him those advantages which are the sure reason of professional distinction.*

Indeed, he had earned respect in many quarters, respect that would ensure him a successful career. This was just as well, as he was to have more than himself to consider in the future: he was now a married man.

Chapter Five
DOMESTIC INTERLUDE

T he story begins while Locke was still at work on the Liverpool & Manchester Railway. While living in Liverpool he continued the process of self-education, in his own words 'to make up the shortcomings of linguistic training at Barnsley Grammar School.' He attended lectures at the Philosophical Institution in Liverpool, where his enthusiasm attracted the attention of the eminent historian William Roscoe. He gave Locke one of his books in 1827 and received a formal reply, indicating that young Joseph was taking his 'linguistic training' seriously: 'I acknowledge with gratitude the presentation of your late work, and I am sure that I shall divine those advantages which the enlightened observations contained in it are calculated to produce. It gives me great pleasure in being thought worthy of your kind attention.'

Roscoe, as well as being a historian, was also a radical and, living in Liverpool, saw at first hand the evils of the slave trade. The anti-slavery poem *The Dying Negro* was printed in Liverpool by John McCreery and Roscoe became a patron of the printer, entrusting him with the printing of his major work, a life of Lorenzo de Medici. McCreery was born in Ireland in 1768, set up in Liverpool, but later tried to make a living in London. It was not a very successful venture and he returned to Liverpool. He was more than just a printer; he was a great enthusiast for the craft of print and celebrated his craft in verse. He wrote and published a long poem, *The Press,* in which he extolled fine craft printing and decried cheaper methods, early forms of mass production. He was particularly enthusiastic about the work of the printer John Baskerville, the designer of the elegant typeface that has his name: he was less enthusiastic about his hometown of Birmingham.

> *When Birmingham – for riots and for crimes*
> *Shall meet the long reproach of future times*
> *Then shall she find amongst our honor'd race*
> *One name to save her from entire disgrace.*

His passion for the art of printing was not just celebrated in the words he wrote, but the whole lengthy poem was intended to display his own typographical gifts. It was embellished by illustrations by the master of woodcuts, Thomas Bewick. The words may be less than inspiring, but the production was magnificent. He was clearly a printer who had mastered his craft, but unfortunately was less successful in managing his business affairs. He relied very heavily on Roscoe's patronage.

He not only wrote for publication, but also provided verses for his own family, including a poem for his younger daughter, Phoebe, on her birthday:

> *A Father's love to thee inclines,*
> *And sends thee, babe, these birth-day lines;*
> *But oh! What can I wish thee more*
> *Than blessings I have called before?-*
> *May still, to thee, this happy day*
> *The purest joys of life convey!*
> *And time extend thee length of years,*
> *Blest with the worth that life endears!*
> *With gentle soul and heart sincere*
> *Be only to thyself severe.*

Yet it appears that friends and family thought Phoebe was unlikely to live a long and happy life, for she was plagued by ill health. It is uncertain what was exactly wrong with her, but Joseph Locke's nephew described her as 'a partially paralysed invalid.'

She must, however, have had her attractions. When Joseph was introduced to her father by Roscoe, he would no doubt have been pleased to meet a meticulous craftsman, but it was the daughter who soon became the main attraction for his visits. At this stage in his career, while still a lowly assistant engineer, there was no question of his being able to propose marriage. But two events changed their relative situations dramatically.

In 1831, McCreery took his wife and his two daughters, Sarah and Phoebe, to Paris. Early the next year, there was an outbreak of cholera in the city and McCreery was one of the many victims. The grieving women returned to England and he was buried in Kensal Green cemetery in London. The death of the father did nothing to diminish Joseph's love of Phoebe. We know little about the young woman, but if she was already showing signs of serious ill health, there must have been a great deal in her character to appeal to the young engineer. Her background was cultured and it is clear from the little poem quoted above that she had a loving father. The courtship seemed destined to go on for a long time, but then Locke's situation changed dramatically when he was employed by the Grand Junction. In the autumn of 1833 he was able to record in a letter that 'The directors have given me a salary of £800 a year, besides about £200 for expenses: this is beyond my expectations in every way.' It was more than enough to clear the way for marriage, and the wedding took place in 1835. They were a young couple, he was twenty-eight and she was twenty-two. Phoebe's mother and sister moved to Richmond, Surrey, to be near to them as they set up house in the London area.

Joseph's biographer Devey noted that in the previous year Joseph had been far from his usual energetic self. 'Whether it was that stress had caused him momentarily to relax his previous efforts, or that the opposition which he met with from his chief had somewhat disenchanted and disgusted him, certain it is that a most intimate friend and acute observer noticed about this period symptoms of slackened energy.' It is not too surprising to find him depressed by the breakdown in relationship with the man who had been his mentor and who he had so admired. How serious his depression was will never be known, but what is certain is that marriage lifted him out of it. It may have been partly due to his improved circumstances, but Devey suggests that a lot of the improvement was due to Phoebe. 'He had fortunately become united with one who was as prompt in spurring his ambitions as in solacing his fatigue.' They remained a happy couple until his death when, against all expectations, Phoebe survived him.

Joseph and Phoebe never had children, but in 1848 they adopted an infant, Minna Maurice, who soon became Minna Locke and was always referred to as 'our daughter'. The picture we have of family life is sketchy, but there is nothing to suggest that Joseph and Phoebe were anything other than a happy couple and she must have had a degree of stoicism to cope with both her disabilities and a husband whose work constantly took him away from home.

Chapter Six
THE LONDON AND SOUTHAMPTON RAILWAY

E ven before work on the Liverpool & Manchester Railway had been completed, work was advancing on other lines in the region. The main line was joined by a branch to Wigan, which in turn was followed by plans for a further extension from Wigan to Preston. The two lines were then amalgamated to create the North Union Railway. Other companies were also looking for future developments, and, as a result, engineers of proven ability were in great demand. Locke was now very definitely one of those men. He had already worked with Charles Vignoles to produce plans for a line from Manchester to the Manchester, Bolton & Bury Canal, and Vignoles himself was to go on to become Chief Engineer for the North Union. It was all a great flurry of activity, with rival schemes all attempting to find their place in the profitable expansion.

While all this was going on, the proprietors of the Grand Junction began to think in terms of expansion north, with a line to Scotland. They asked Locke to survey a possible route and report on its feasibility. He set off to journey over the northern fells to the Southern Uplands across the border and duly put in his report – *The London and Glasgow Railway through Lancashire* in 1836. It was not exactly an in-depth study, running to just three pages in the printed edition. For whatever reason, the Grand Junction directors were in no hurry to push onward across the border. However, with connections now made to Preston, it seemed sensible to move on even further north to Lancaster. In 1836 Locke was asked to survey the route and he produced two reports, as a result of which he was invited to take on the job of Chief Engineer, which he accepted.

By this time, Locke's reputation was assured as a safe pair of hands, a man who could bring a line in on time and on or even under budget. He put in his estimate for the total cost at £250,000, a very modest £12,500 per mile. To put this in perspective, the Dublin & Kingston

Railway, opened in 1834 and just 6 miles long, had cost a staggering £50,000 per mile. Needless to say, the directors were greatly cheered when they saw the figures and anticipated substantial profits. Things did not go quite as planned. Building the line presented few problems; the whole route lay along the flat coastal plain. It was an obvious line, following the existing turnpike road and closely copied in more recent times by the M6. It was so straightforward that the busy young engineer felt confident enough to hand over most of the supervison to an assistant. Then the troubles started. They began when the government insisted that the planned bridges were inadequate: they had to be built higher and with more substantial abutments. Then the tricky business of land purchase brought new difficulties. £25,000 had been allowed for this; in the event the cost rose to £90,000.

One important decision that had to be taken was the siting of the terminus. It was decided to build the station in Dock Street close to the Lancaster Canal, in the expectation that there would be a connection with the North Union line. But the latter Company built their station 200 yards away. It was typical of the age that companies were often more concerned with protecting their own interests as they saw them, rather than considering the convenience of passengers. It was a fact of railway construction that Locke was to denounce later in life (see p.90). The two companies that could usefully have co-operated saw themselves more as rivals. Eventually common sense did prevail: the companies were merged, the lines joined and Carlisle residents had just the one station to go to for all their trains.

Taking over the North Union proved, however, something of a mixed blessing. Vignoles had rather overestimated the power of locomotives available to work the line. He had more difficult country to work in than Locke but was quite prepared to take a direct line up quite steep slopes, and the tough gradient on the stretch of line running to the west of Chorley was particularly demanding. It was said that in the early days the guard often had to call for help from passengers to get out and help give the engine a shove to get it started up the bank: the request only went to the third class. Even without the need to get out and push it was notoriously slow and it was not unknown for passengers who just missed a train to be encouraged to trot after it and clamber aboard.

Locke may have exceeded his original budget as the final cost was

£400,000 not the estimated £250,000. The directors must have been disappointed to find the man they had chosen for his ability to keep down costs had not managed to do so. They could, however, console themselves with the thought that it was still cheaper than any other railway under construction at that time. The cost of £20,000 was still less than half that of the Dublin & Kingston Railway and compared very favourably with the neighbouring North Union at £30,000. And it was still cheaper than Locke's earlier Grand Junction, though that was only to be expected given the difference in engineering work involved. The miscalculation did nothing to dent Locke's reputation as a sound man who could be relied on to get things done competently, on time and at low cost.

Joseph Locke had come a long way from the happy-go-lucky boy who had skipped in and out of a variety of jobs before having had the immense good fortune of being taken under the wing of George Stephenson. That he had been forced to disagree with his mentor had undoubtedly cast a dark shadow over the life of the young man, but now he had no need to rely on his association with any more experienced engineer; he had earned his own place in the world. His status was confirmed in February 1838 when he was elected as a Fellow of the Royal Society, the country's most prestigious scientific organisation. It seems a little odd to us today as, whatever his achievements might have been, he would hardly be considered nowadays as having advanced science in any way, or even at this stage made any important new contribution to technology apart from the introduction of the double-headed rail. Those who proposed him were mostly other engineers, including Brunel and Rastrick. There was one scientist among the nominees, Dr Dionysius Lardner, who is mostly famous these days for very unscientific predictions: steamships could never cross the Atlantic and travelling through Box tunnel by train would inevitably prove fatal. The reasons given for proposing him seemed to rest on his work on the Grand Junction and for being 'a gentleman well conversant with every aspect of practical science.' What makes it even more surprising is that no similar honour had yet been offered to Robert Stephenson, who with the design of *Rocket* had transformed locomotive development. Those involved must have known of Locke's falling out with George Stephenson and this could have been their way of showing their support for the careful approach to construction contracts as opposed to the rather slapdash methods of the older man. Robert Stephenson finally got the initial F.R.S. behind his name in 1849.

While Locke was still at work in the northwest, a number of Lancashire investors had put money into a new line from London to Southampton. The idea had first been mooted in 1830. There were several reasons why the line was thought desirable. The Napoleonic Wars were still fresh in the memory and there were many who saw Southampton as the ideal deep-sea port as the entrance to the Solent could easily be protected from attack from the sea. At that time packet boats from the continent were mostly docking at Falmouth, which meant there was a long, slow land journey before despatches could reach London. Devey spelled out other advantages:

Then there were the Torbay fisheries, the produce of which was often found rotting in Southampton for want of a speedy communication with London; and the merchant vessels, which instead of discharging their cargoes at an opportune harbour, were obliged to pass round the North Foreland; and proceed at a snail's pace up the blockaded Thames.

He went on to suggest that Southampton could also be the major port for vessels from the Far East, bringing 'the jewels of Delhi and the silks of Cashmere.' There was only one problem: although Southampton had been an important port since Roman times, it lacked modern facilities, so the original proposal included provision for building a new dock complex. A prospectus for the Southampton, London & Branch Railway & Dock Company was duly issued; the branch referred to was one that was planned to run from the main line towards Bath and Bristol. Francis Giles was appointed as the engineer to survey the route for the proposed main line. He was a very experienced engineer, born in 1787, who had been trained as a surveyor and spent the earlier part of his working life with the elder John Rennie. He had been involved in a number of important canal projects and, no doubt influenced by the Rennie connection, he was among those who were opposed to George Stephenson's appointment to the Liverpool & Manchester and famously remarked that 'no engineer in his senses would go through Chat Moss if he wanted to make a railway from Liverpool to Manchester.' He prophesied that even if a line were constructed, the first locomotive that tried to use it would sink to the bottom of the bog. Perhaps his rather conservative and cautious outlook made him seem an ideal candidate for the role of Chief Engineer for the proposed line. He was, in any case, one of the few engineers who already had railway experience, thanks to his work in the construction of the Newcastle & Carlisle.

The first survey completed, the original promoters felt able to raise the capital to go to Parliament and Giles set off again to do a second survey to meet the more rigorous demands of the official application for an Act. In the event, the decision was taken to hold back on bringing forward their Bill until after the London & Birmingham Bill had been approved, reasoning that if that major trunk route from London went through, there would be an easier passage for the next route from the capital. This was indeed the case, but they were no longer alone in thinking of lines to the south west from London: Brunel's Great Western put in an appearance and effectively scuppered the originally proposed branch line. It was also decided that dock development should be left to a separate company, so the only line now would be the main line.

The Act was duly obtained and work began under Giles in 1834. The route was well chosen. The most direct route was made impossible by the great swelling rise of the South Downs that lay right across the potential track. Instead, the route headed out west through Wimbledon and on to Weybridge and Basingstoke, before heading south for Winchester and Southampton. The London terminus was south of the river at Nine Elms, a site now occupied by the new Covent Garden flower market. There were four tunnels on the line: two of them were very close together and the most demanding to build, three quarters of a mile and 200 yards respectively at Popham Beacon, between Basingstoke and Winchester. The most troublesome works proposed in the plan, however, turned out not to be in tunnelling but in creating a deep cutting through the chalk at St George's Hill near Weybridge. This proposal provided an opportunity to reverse a previous argument: now it was George Stephenson's turn to produce scathing criticism of the cutting that would be over a hundred feet below the surface at its deepest point. Relationships between Giles and the Stephensons had never been very good; and Giles had already suffered the indignity of failing to gain the job of Chief Engineer for the London & Birmingham Railway, which had gone to young Robert. In the event, it was the Stephenson camp that triumphed, with success at Chat Moss and on the London to Birmingham line, while Giles was floundering on the new route to Southampton.

Giles, like many engineers of the time, had more than one project on the go when he started on the London & Southampton line. That should not have been a problem, but he had made a fundamental mistake in parcelling up the works between a large number of small contractors. It was impossible for him to keep strict control over all of them and it seems that, left to their own devices, they did the easy work first and began to try to renegotiate contracts when things got more difficult. Work proceeded at an incredibly slow pace: in the first year only 2 miles of track had been completed and by early 1836, after nearly two years of work, the figure had only risen to 10 miles. There was increasing discontent among the shareholders, who felt that not only was the work going slowly, but was already showing signs of going over budget. A group led by the Lancashire investors, who were by now used to seeing construction carried out efficiently, protested. They called on the man they knew they could trust and sent Joseph Locke off to survey the works. His report could never have been other than critical. Giles resigned before he was pushed and, by the beginning of 1837, Locke was appointed as the new Chief Engineer.

The line was notable for its use of 'cut and fill', with the spoil from cuttings being used to build embankments. This was particularly the case in the section between Basingstoke and Winchester that crossed the edge of the South Downs. This section was entrusted to the man who had proved himself on the Grand Junction, Thomas Brassey. In his biography of Brassey, published in 1872, Sir Arthur Helps discussed the relationship between the two men:

> *It has been thought by some persons that Mr. Locke showed a spirit of favouritism for Mr. Brassey; and this is so far true, that Mr. Locke was always delighted to have Mr. Brassey as a coadjutor; but those who knew anything of the qualities of that eminent engineer, Mr. Locke, must be well aware that his regard as a man of business for any other man of business would have been founded upon no prejudices, and upon no unreasonable favouritism. To put the matter plainly, it was soon discovered that whenever Mr. Brassey had undertaken a contract on a line, the Engineer-in-chief had but little occasion for rigid supervision. Mr. Locke well knew that a*

bargain once concluded with Mr. Brassey would be exactly, I may say handsomely, fulfilled, and that no difficulties or contingencies would be made an excuse for delay, or an occasion for demanding any alterations in the terms of the contract.

It was precisely because Locke had contractors who could be relied on to carry out his own carefully detailed instructions, which included a number of variations on the original route, that made his method of working so much more efficient than Giles. One of his first decisions was to reroute the line to avoid the deep St George's cutting and it could well be that other important changes were made. One nineteenth-century report states that the line was originally laid using stone-sleeper blocks, but that was later changed to wooden sleepers. If that is the case, then we can assume that the older technique was employed by Giles and Locke would have changed to the new technology he had used on the Grand Junction. He also seems to have increased the weight of rail used. In evidence to a committee investigating 'the deterioration of railway stock and road' of 1843, he spoke firmly in favour of wooden sleepers and also gave his views on the appropriate weight of rail. He noted that the Liverpool & Manchester Railway had initially been laid with rail weighing just 35lbs/yard, but that had been increased over the years to 75lbs/yard and he regarded that figure as perfectly adequate for double-headed rails. This was his likeliest choice for the London & Southampton track. As a result of his rerouting to avoid the deepest cutting and other improvements, he was able to tell the directors that the route would be open from London to Woking by 1 May 1838. He was as good as his word: the line was completed and once the official inspection had shown everything was in order, the directors set off from Nine Elms on 12 May and ended their journey 23 miles away at Woking Common. It was a more than ample vindication of the decision to replace Giles. The line was at once opened for business, and the Company were keen to make the most of their opportunities. Derby Day was only two weeks after the opening run and advertisements were placed for race day special trains. The effect was rather more than they had bargained for:

A crowd of about 5,000 persons were found at the station gates. Several trains were despatched but still the throng increased, till at length, and amid the shrieks of the female portion of their number, the mob broke over the booking counter, leaped through the windows, invaded the platform and rushed pell mell into a train chartered by a private party. Finding resistance useless, the official sent for the Metropolitan Police and at twelve o'clock a notice was posted in the booking office window announcing that no more trains would run that day.

It was a promising beginning, if not too promising. Doubts must have arisen about having a London terminus with a single platform. But there were inevitable delays in the work on the troublesome section south of Basingstoke, particularly with earth movement on the banks and cuttings, problems that plagued many early railway engineers, just as they had their canal predecessors. For a time this section had to be covered by stage coaches linking the completed part of this sections with the line running north from Southampton. Even so the whole line was declared officially open on 11 May 1840. This was no mean achievement considering Giles had only managed to oversee completion of ten miles in two years. Locke had been forced to revise the budget when he took command, raising it from one million to £1,507, 753. In the end, when all the costs were added up, the final bill came to £1,551, 914, a very modest overspend for a major project.

With the route to Southampton completed, the decision was taken to extend the network with a branch to Portsmouth. However, the notion that the home of the Royal Navy should somehow be served by no more than a branch line from a mere mercantile marine port was clearly unacceptable to the locals. Portsmouth, they felt, deserved better, and they opened new negotiations with the London & Brighton Company as offering a possible alternative route to the capital. In the event the proposed line to Portsmouth failed to raise the necessary funds, and instead the London & Southampton Company promoted a simpler route to Gosport, and the Act of 1839 authorised a change of name to the London & South Western Railway, which placated local feelings. It was the start of what was to become a major network over the coming years.

Once again Locke was the Chief Engineer and Brassey his contractor. It should all have been fairly straightforward but the work did involve the construction of a tunnel at Fareham. This was built through clay and just before the planned opening in July 1841 a major landslip occurred. Repairing the damage was severely hampered by long periods of heavy rain and, in spite of the best efforts of Locke and the contractor, the opening was delayed until November of that year. However, the works had still not stabilised, and a further landslip caused a closure and a reopening in February 1842. It was an embarrassment to Locke, who prided himself on bringing in his work on time and on budget, but the consequences for Brassey were even more severe. He was, as ever, prepared to stick by the terms of his original contract, and as a result was almost made bankrupt. The station at Gosport was a very grand affair, and from there passengers could take a chain ferry across the water to Portsmouth.

The completion of the railway provided a great boost for the docks at Southampton. Paddle steamers were now making the crossing to Le Havre and the opening of a brand new dock in 1843 brought more deep-sea shipping to the port. It was a development aided by Locke's work – and in the near future he would also be a beneficiary. In the meantime, there were other lines in Britain demanding his attention.

Chapter Seven
THE GREAT TUNNEL

Many schemes were being proposed in the years following the success of the Liverpool & Manchester Railway, one of which, for a line linking Manchester to Sheffield, has a history that goes back even further in time. This was always going to be a problematical route, as a glance at an Ordnance Survey map will easily demonstrate. The two towns, not at that date cities, are separated by the Peak National Park, a sparsely populated region of the Pennines dominated by high, peaty moorland. The first proposed line was set out by the man of the moment, George Stephenson. It avoided the worst of the high ground, the bleak expanses of Hallam and Burbage Moors, by taking a route to the south via Hathersage. Even so, the line as laid out contained 6½ miles of tunnels in a 43-mile route and several gradients that could only have been worked by stationary engines and cable haulage. In spite of the difficulties, an Act for the Sheffield & Manchester Railway was obtained in 1831, authorising capital of £530,000. There was widespread criticism of the whole concept and the scheme had to be abandoned.

In 1835 a group of prominent citizens from Sheffield, Manchester and the towns of Ashton-under-Lyne and Stalybridge, headed by Lord Wharncliffe, revived the idea and formed a new company, the Sheffield, Ashton-under-Lyne and Manchester Railway. Charles Vignoles was invited to provide plans for a new route and Locke was also involved, though it was mainly in order to offer a critique of the senior engineer's work. Vignoles' route was described in the document put out by the committee:

> It is intended that the station at Manchester shall be in or near Store Street, and from thence the Railway will proceed by Gorton, Woodhead, Ashton-under-Lyne (with a very short branch to Staley Bridge), Hyde, Glossop, Woodhead, Turleston, Penistone and Wortley to the Town of Sheffield.

There was to be a 2-mile long tunnel under the Pennines and the whole line could be worked by locomotives. Locke basically approved the route, but had variations of his own to propose. There was a certain amount of bickering by the Committee, some of whom preferred Locke's ideas to Vignoles', which tried the patience of both men. Eventually, the route was finalised, with some changes. The line was now to be 40¾ miles long, with Glossop and Stalybridge now served by branch lines. The most important change was the lengthening of the summit tunnel, which was to be extended from 2 miles to 3 miles, reducing the summit level to 943 feet and ensuring that gradients on the main line could be kept no steeper than 1 in 120. The need for stationary engines had gone: the whole route could now be worked by locomotives.

Locke's report had been far-sighted, pointing out the advantages of having a line that would promote the development of the rich and extensive South Yorkshire coalfield: 'the great, I may say the greatest, unworked coalfield in England.' He also envisaged an eventual extension eastwards towards the Humber, bringing grain from Lincolnshire to the rapidly developing industrial towns of northern England and allowing manufactured goods to be sent to the east coast.

Vignoles' report was a model of clarity and utterly convincing in its arguments. He pointed out that it was essential that the Chief Engineer should have the complete backing and trust of the investors, and that this was particularly necessary when the route contained imposing viaducts and the longest railway tunnel yet planned. But, he also pointed out that seeing a job well and efficiently done was as much in the engineer's interest as anyone's: 'he must build up his reputation as much, if not more, upon the economy with which his designs may be executed as, than upon their merits. In this country, an Engineer's Career in his profession depends mainly on the success of the works as commercial enterprises.' This was a statement with which Locke would have whole-heartedly agreed: he built his entire career on just such a premise. Vignoles then went on to lay out in detail how he proposed to proceed with the work.

First of all, he said, the whole line had to be laid out 'with geometrical accuracy' and for that to be done in the wild countryside of The Peak would probably take a year. After that, the lengthy process of negotiating to purchase the land should begin and, while that continued, work should start on the great tunnel. As originally envisaged this was to be dug by sinking eleven shafts at equal intervals along the line, the deepest of which would be sunk 600 feet below the surface. He had consulted with local engineers from the Derbyshire lead mines and he was sure that they would cost an average of £500 per shaft, not counting the costs of any pumping engines that might be needed. There would, he declared, be no problem in attracting skilled workers:

I conceive there will be no difficulty in the Country as there are many Gangs of Working Miners as will enable the whole number of shafts to be worked at once, first building huts on the Hills for the men; a measure absolutely necessary for the absence of all accommodation for them otherwise.

He estimated that it would be possible to sink 7 yards a week and once the bottom level was reached, exploratory small tunnels could be worked to determine the nature of the ground. The final optimistic forecast was that once the shareholders who had raised the initial finance saw how well things were progressing, there would be no trouble finding the funds to complete the work.

He also forecast that locomotives would be found 'which will be able to travel with four or five passenger carriages, averaging 18 or 20 passengers each between the two great Towns in about two hours and a half', while goods trains could haul 60-ton loads in three and a half hours. As the first plan only called for a 2-mile tunnel, the trip through would only take ten minutes and the whole tunnel would be lit by lanterns to make it less terrifying. It all sounded wonderfully logical, but somehow or other the potential investors remained largely unmoved. In order to get work started, Vignoles bought a large body of shares himself and persuaded friends and relatives to invest, while standing surety for them. He did so on the basis of a verbal understanding with Lord Wharncliffe, the company's Chairman, that if extra funds were needed, there would be no further call on his shares or those of his associates. All his optimistic forecasts and intentions were to fail to materialise.

Work finally got under way on 1 October 1838, with the ceremonial cutting of the first sods at a site near the western entrance to the proposed Woodhead tunnel. The first sod was cut by Lord Wharncliffe, the next by Vignoles and then the rest of the directors took their turn with the spade. According to the report in the *Manchester Guardian*, 'The ladies, whom the difficulty of descent prevented them forming part of the group, witnessed this ceremony from a neighbouring knoll, and appeared much amused with the awkward performance of some of the Directors and young men.' It was arguably the last amusing event to occur on that windswept moor.

As funds were scarce, to save time it was decided to build a first tunnel to take a single track. It would be just over 3 miles long, and work would be carried out from just five shafts, the deepest at 600 feet and with an average depth of 450 feet. Work could also start from the portals at either end. Once the shafts were sunk, twelve teams of men could be used, two working in either direction from the bottoms of the shafts and the remainder working inwards from the ends. With such large gaps, good surveying techniques were essential if the different sections were to meet, something which both Locke and Vignoles were acutely aware of from their work on the Liverpool & Manchester tunnels.

As anyone who has ever walked the Peak District in winter will know, conditions can be extremely harsh, hence Vignoles' insistence that the men should be provided with properly built huts. It never happened. Instead, the Company reluctantly sent tents to relieve the men, who at first were sleeping out in the open. Contracts were handed out, but on a piecemeal basis. The Company was reluctant to release funds, largely because the coffers were low from lack of subscriptions. Work stuttered on, instead of proceeding in the speedy orderly manner anticipated by the Chief Engineer. Progress was not helped by the fact that there were three committees representing the interests of the two termini and one on the middle. They argued among themselves and interfered with the engineering: it was not unknown for a committee member with no engineering experience whatsoever to arrive at the tunnel workings and give orders to the men, contrary to the engineer's instructions. Not surprisingly, it was soon necessary to make a call on the existing shareholders for more money.

In spite of the agreement with the chairman, Vignoles was asked to make further payment on his shares. He appealed to Lord Wharncliffe for help and offered to relinquish his existing shares, provided that the matter was then declared closed. Wharncliffe agreed, pointing out that he was being asked to find a further £140,000 over and above his initial investment: 'I know that gentleman can no more pay that than I can pay the national debt.' On 15 May 1839, Vignoles retired. In his diary he wrote: 'Thus ends my connection with the Sheffield & Manchester Railway, after great attention bestowed on it for nearly four years, and having sustained on its account, in one shape or another, an actual loss of £10,000 in hard monies.' Worse was to follow: the Company sued him for the call on his shares and he lost the High Court action. 'Good God!,' he wrote, 'that men whom I have served so faithfully, and for whose railway I had done so much, should act like this!' Lord Wharncliffe did the honourable thing and also resigned from the Company that had behaved so shoddily.

There was now only one obvious candidate to take over the work: Joseph Locke. Given his well-known aversion to tunnels in general, he must at least have had some doubts about taking on the biggest of them all and one that had to be built in a terrible environment. Nevertheless, he accepted the challenge and duly took over as Chief Engineer. His first step was to rationalise the haphazard system of letting out the works to a series of small contractors. The work on the tunnel was divided between two contractors: Richard Hattersley was given the western end and Thomas Nicholson the eastern. The Resident Engineer, William Purdon, who had worked for Vignoles, was kept on in his job and was to be the only engineer who worked on the line from start to finish. The tunnel was notorious for the high rate of injuries and deaths among the navvies, and although the rate of injuries dropped after the new contractors took over it remained distressingly high: in all 32 men were killed, 200 were severely injured and a further 400 received minor injuries. The official records do not include those who suffered from serious and even fatal diseases, largely caused by the insanitary conditions in which the men were forced to live. Inevitably, the contractors had to offer higher wages than normal to persuade anyone to take on work at Woodhead.

Locke had to take ultimate responsibility for the working conditions at Woodhead, but he faced a dilemma. He had already had to break the bad news to the cash-strapped committee that the original estimates for the tunnel were hopelessly low. Vignoles had allowed £106,000: Locke estimated the cost at £207,000. The only way the costs could be recouped was from revenue once the line was open. The pressure was on for Locke to finish the job both as quickly and as cheaply as possible.

That was his prime consideration and these requirements had repercussions on the works at Woodhead.

Conditions had been bad from the first. Devey described the first problem:

The difficulties of getting provisions to the place proved almost as great as victualling Balaklava. There is no town of any description for ten miles off, and provisions having to be dragged up a steep acclivity could not be sold at any price the navvies could afford to pay. The contractors had to open shops of their own, and pay their men partly in food.

Devey was more than a little disingenuous. A Manchester surgeon, John Robertson, visited the site in 1841, long after Locke had taken on overall responsibility, and reported in length on the conditions that he found. Far from offering food at prices the navvies could afford, the contractors were operating what were known as Tommy shops. The men were given tickets they could exchange for food, but prices were generally more than 50 per cent higher than those in Manchester. On site, potatoes, for example, that could be bought for eight pence a score, cost six pence more on site, an increase of 75 per cent. Matters were made even worse by the fact that the men were only paid once every two months – according to Devey again, this was to prevent 'hebdomadal excesses', in other words to prevent them getting drunk every week. But in practice, though the Tommy tickets for food were only issued at specified regular intervals, to ensure that all workers had enough to eat to keep their strength up, beer tickets were available at any time. Robertson discovered the pernicious effects of this system. A man could take a five-shilling ticket to the beer shop, where beer was available at sixpence a quart. He could get drunk and then be told he had spent all his ticket – as this would have meant he had consumed twenty pints it was unlikely to be true, but the unhappy man was in no condition to argue. Drunkenness was unquestionably a contributory factor to the accident rate, but it was not the whole story.

The work itself was arduous and inherently dangerous. Most of the material through which the tunnel had to be bored was millstone grit, a form of sandstone, which as its name suggests was so hard that it could be used for grindstones in mills. The men had to drill holes into this tough material by hand, then pack the holes with gunpowder to blow the rock apart. In 1846, Parliament set up a Committee on the Conditions of Labourers, and among those who were examined was the Resident Engineer at Woodhead, William Purdon. There were two particular lines of questioning. The first dealt with the stemmers, which were used to pack the powder into the drilled holes, after which the ends were plugged with clay. At Woodhead, iron stemmers were used, and if in the process the iron hit the rock and caused a spark, there could be an instant explosion. An alternative was available, copper stemmers, but Purdon did not use them. The Committee took a dim view of this:

'You thought, on the part of the company, that it was worth while running the risk of two or three men's lives rather than go to the expense of more expensive tools?'

'You must prove that any man's life was lost.'

The Committee then referred to a pamphlet produced by none other than the contractor Thomas Nicholson, and read out the following extract:

'William Jackson, miner No.5 shaft. He was looking over John Webb's shoulder, while he was stemming a hole charged with powder, when the blast went off, blowing the stemmer through Jackson's head and killing him instantly.'

To which the only reply Purdon could make, was: 'the copper stemmers are very soft in the head, that they are objectionable.'

The Committee then moved on to another aspect of blasting. To light the charge, the usual procedure was to insert a rod into the clay plug, withdraw it, fill the hole and create a trail of powder. The man given that task would light the trail then scamper to the shaft to be hauled out of harm's way. Things did not always go according to plan. In other evidence, the Committee heard how at Box tunnel and on the Great Western Railway, the cage had jammed in the shaft, and the man was just able to scramble out in time to shut off the powder trail before he was blown to smithereens. There was an alternative available, the safety fuse. This had been invented by William Buckford in 1831 and consisted of a varnished cord with a core of gunpowder that burned slowly and, more importantly, at a constant rate. The Committee suggested that this had to be safer than the method used at Woodhead, to which Purdon replied, 'Perhaps it is, but it is attended with much loss of time, and the difference is so very small, I would not recommend the loss of time for the sake of all the extra lives it would save.'

How far Purdon's views represented those of the Chief Engineer we have no means of knowing, but Locke's philosophy of the importance of moving work along as fast and as cheaply as possible, without actually jeopardising the engineering works, may well have played a part. The dangers from explosions were not the only perils faced by the tunnellers. Although gritstone predominated, the workers often ran into areas of loose shale, where rock falls were all too common. And whatever section was being worked, the conditions were bad. Water was a constant problem – Locke had to bring in more powerful pumps than had been allowed for in Vignoles' plans. Even so, the floor of the tunnel was always thick with mud, through which the men had to struggle to remove the rubble. The men were required to work day and night, including Sundays, much to the disgust of the non-conformist ministers who made the trek up to the workings to do what they could for the men.

In spite of all the difficulties, work on the tunnel was completed in December 1845. On the 20th, a party consisting of General Pasley, the Government Inspector of Railways, Locke and his staff and a group of directors made the first trip through Woodhead tunnel. The *Manchester Guardian* reported the event:

On going through the tunnel, the general was preceded in the train by a wagon bearing the men with torches, which were held to the roof and sides, the train proceeding very slowly so that the nature of the work might be closely and carefully examined, and we understand that General Pasley expressed his entire satisfaction with the work generally, and indeed declared that it was one of the finest pieces of engineering he had ever seen.

A triumph it may have been, but it was only built to take a single track, and it was clear that would not be enough for a main line, joining two such important towns as Sheffield and Manchester. During construction, the plans had allowed for two-foot deep drainage ditches to be cut, and a total of twenty-five arches were inserted at roughly 200-yard intervals into the side walls. Locke, at least, must have been aware that a single-track tunnel would be a bottleneck and had planned accordingly. It was just as well, as it was soon apparent that the tunnel presented special problems, particularly the need to prevent accidents on the single track.

A pilot engine was kept permanently at the tunnel and no train could proceed without it. This engine had a powerful, oil-burning Argand lamp set at the front to shine a light down the tunnel – Vignoles' tunnel lamps never materialised. There was also a very up to date addition: a telegraph wire was slung down the length of the tunnel.

The first Woodhead tunnel was an engineering triumph. The care with which the original survey had been carried out was demonstrated when the first drifts were dug from the bottoms of the shafts, and were found to meet within a few inches of each other. It was also a monumental task. No accurate figures for the numbers employed on the work exist, but it has been reliably estimated that at times as many as a thousand and possibly more were at work at any one time. Other statistics are equally impressive. To keep the workings at least moderately dry, eight million tons of water were pumped out; 157 tons of gunpowder were used for blasting and almost 300,000 cubic yards of material were excavated. But it all came at a human cost. One of the most telling comments came from a missionary sent to the navvies from Salford, who described an encounter in his journal:

> *Going over the moor, this morning, met two women. One said, 'Have you not sometimes been to pray for Johnson?' I said I had. 'He is dead', said she; 'I have just laid him out; it is but little more than six years since I came here to live in these hills, and he is the twenty-ninth man I have laid out, and the first of them who died a natural death.'*

It has to be said, however, that the Woodhead tunnel was exceptionally difficult to build, and was by no means the only tunnel which was finished at a high cost in lives. At Otley, in Yorkshire, there is a monument in the churchyard, one of the very few commemorating railway navvies. It is dedicated to the men who died constructing the Bramhope tunnel on the Leeds & Thirsk Railway. It was two thirds the length of Woodhead, but the memorial is for the twenty-three men who died in its construction.

While work continued on the tunnel, the rest of the line was being built. There were two major structures, the viaducts at Etherow and Dinting Vale. Both were designed by Locke using timber, soaked in copper sulphate solution as a preservative, and mounted on masonry piers. They were imposing structures: Etherow was 506ft long and 136ft high and carried on three arches: Dinting Vale, 1,455ft long and 121ft high on five arches. In 1859, the timber superstructure was replaced by wrought-iron box girders.

Once the inspectorate had approved Woodhead tunnel, the whole line could be opened and the official ceremony took place on 22 December 1845, no doubt to the great relief of the shareholders who had never expected that more than seven years would have passed since the first sod had been cut. A special train loaded with dignitaries left Sheffield in the morning and, as the passengers emerged from the gloom of Woodhead, they gave three cheers, either as acknowledgement of the achievement or in relief at having got safely through. On arrival at Manchester they were greeted by a band playing what was the obligatory tune on such occasions, Handel's *See the Conquering Hero Comes*. There followed the equally usual banquet and speeches. The line was finally completed and open for business.

Very little is known about the three locomotives ordered at the start, other than the fact they were built by Kirtley & Co. The carriages were of the usual variety – comfortable, first class; rather less comfortable second class, and third class that was little better than open trucks, in which passengers were expected to stand. Travelling through the more or less unventilated Woodhead tunnel as third-class passengers must have been a decidedly uncomfortable experience, as the choking smoke from the engine drifted over them. But then, they were not much worse off than the driver and fireman on their open footplate.

It was not long, however, before the need for a second tunnel at Woodhead became essential for the efficient running of the line. Work began in 1847 and was made far simpler than the original workings had been. Access was through the side arches, so no deep shafts had to be sunk, and the underlying geology was by now more clearly understood. There were far fewer accidents, but there was one disastrous period. In 1849, the men had been working day and night shifts and when in May they finally got paid, many went off on a prolonged drinking bout over the Whitsun holiday. When they returned to the workings, many were ill and the *Manchester Guardian* put the illness down to 'the grossest imprudence and intemperance'. It was far more serious: it was cholera and twenty-five men died. They were not the only casualties: two of the nurses who had volunteered to help the doctors at the site also died from the outbreak. For a time, all work came to a halt as the navvies deserted their huts to avoid the sickness. Eventually, as the epidemic ended, work resumed, and the second tunnel was opened in February 1852.

The Woodhead tunnels had an evil reputation, partly because of the great suffering involved in their construction, and partly because travel through those smoke-choked bores was always an unpleasant experience. Some indication of just how smoky they were came in the 1960s, when it was decided to run power cables through the second tunnel. Workers had to remove soot deposits two inches thick from the brick lining. By this date, the two original tunnels had closed, replaced by a wider tunnel with double tracks. Construction on that began in 1949. Using the most modern machinery, it took four years to complete, which makes the work on Locke's original tunnel, where everything was done by hand, an even more remarkable achievement.

Chapter Eight

CREWE

While work on the Sheffield, Manchester & Ashton-under-Lyne Railway was still making its slow and tortuous progress, Locke was called on once again to turn his attention to his first major project, the Grand Junction. Since the opening of that line, the network had been expanding. As railways became both more common and more popular, investors started looking at ways in which connections could be improved. The Grand Junction had taken advantage of the existing link to the Liverpool & Manchester, but it was not the ideal route to Manchester as it involved joining the latter line and then turning through almost 90 degrees, switching from running in a northerly to an easterly direction. A more obvious line from Birmingham was to head on a much more direct route through the Potteries. That line would be built in time, but not for many years. In the meantime, an alternative route was being promoted by the Manchester & Cheshire Junction Railway. The same awkward 90-degree turn was faced by passengers heading on the Grand Junction for Liverpool. Again, an alternative was available, one which Locke had considered a real possibility even before the Act was passed. He had even foreseen where the most convenient place to make a junction would be – near the hamlet of Monks Coppenhall. But the junction and its station took its name instead from nearby Crewe Hall. The Manchester & Cheshire Junction would also have a connecting branch to Crewe. Both lines were approved by the Manchester & Birmingham and Chester & Crewe Acts of June 1837. The Chester & Crewe Railway was completed in 1840 and two years later the line from Stockport to Crewe was opened. The little rural hamlet was suddenly gaining importance.

The Grand Junction was having problems with maintaining its locomotives and rolling stock. The locomotive repair works were at Edge Hill but there was little room there for expansion, and work on other rolling stock was spread around a number of different depots. The case for having a brand new works in which everything could be carried out at the same site was clear and obvious, as was the best location. It had to be Crewe, where the new works could serve not only the Grand Junction itself, but could cope with the other lines already arriving there – and more that were planned for the future. In 1840 the Board ordered the purchase of a large area of land at Crewe, and gave Locke succinct instructions. He was to prepare plans and estimates 'which shall include the building and repair of carriages and wagons as well as engines.' This was a new departure. Locke explained its significance, writing after the Grand Junction had been absorbed into the larger Company, the London & North Western Railway in 1846:

> *At an early period the Grand Junction Company bought all their locomotives from manufacturers, and it was only justice to admit, that those of Messrs R. Stephenson & Co. were the best. But the engines were, necessarily in need of constant repair, and an establishment was formed for that purpose, at Crewe. Then arose the question, whether this establishment could not be advantageously used, not only for repair, but also for the construction of engines. The plan was tried, and all the engines for the Lancaster & Carlisle, for the northern section of the London & North Western, and for the Chester & Holyhead were built there; and the cost was found to be much less than the price that had been formerly paid.*

Locke appears to be suggesting that the plan for locomotive construction was something of an afterthought, but as his initial instructions quoted above show, the idea was there from the start.

The site chosen occupied 2½ acres (1 hectare) between the lines to Liverpool and Chester. There was no available labour locally, so men had to be brought in for the job and more would be recruited to run the works when they were opened. The effect on the area was felt immediately. The 1841 Census showed the population of Monks Coppenhall as 203: by the end of the following year there were about a thousand living there. It was essential to provide appropriate facilities for those who would eventually man the new works. The Company would need to employ craftsmen. Navvies might be prepared to live in shanty towns and makeshift huts, but not skilled mechanics. So the Company had to provide decent houses for them to live in and proper facilities. In the original plans, spaces were left for the eventual establishment of a church and a school. An architect, John Cunningham was employed to supervise all the work at a salary of £300 a year, and some of the workers' houses he designed survive in the town. These were terraced cottages, of the familiar kind but solidly built of brick on firm stone foundations with slate roofs. Cunningham would no doubt be astonished to discover that the asking price for one of these modest cottages is now in the region of £100,000.

There were four classes of houses. The best were described as being in the 'villa style', built in the fashionable Gothic in blocks of four and intended for 'superior officers' of the Company. The cottages for the labourers were of the familiar two up two down variety. Water was supplied by the Company free of charge, though only the better class had it on tap in their houses; others had to fetch it from a communal tap. Gas was laid on, and charged at the rate of 2d a week per burner. The houses had privies and cesspits, cleared by the Company – who dumped the waste in a nearby stream. The water for the town was collected upstream of the dumping site – contemporary reports have no comments on the effect on anyone unfortunate enough to live downstream.

Water supply was actually something of a problem from the start. Locke ordered a well to be drilled, but when the water began to flow it was found to be salty and the project had to be abandoned. Cheshire was famous for its salt works, so perhaps this is not too surprising. So the brook had to be used. The Company purchased an old grain mill and dam to create a reservoir and erected a steam pump near the locomotive works. This pumped the water through filter beds to a water tower, which supplied both the works and the town.

The Company was paternalistic, providing a wide range of facilities, including a school for the workers' children, supervised by a committee made up of directors' wives. A Mechanics Institute was built and a health service provided. A bath house was soon added to the public buildings. The original plans called for a church to be built, and it was duly constructed. To all appearances it was a typical Victorian church, with attractive marble columns in the nave. But rap one of those columns and instead of a dull, stony thud you get a metallic ping. The Company found it cheaper to cast the columns in iron at the works and paint them to imitate stone. Little now remains of this building apart from the tower.

The grandest buildings in Crewe in the early days were those of the works themselves. A newspaper account of 1846 gave a detailed description:

> *On the right you turn into a large apartment fitted up for building new wagons; it opens into another still larger, and here wagons are repaired. Further on is the forge where the iron work of Mr Owens' department (the wagon-shops) is executed. The fan is used instead of the bellows; but here, as in all the other smithies, bellows are erected in the event of the fan failing. Turning round from the wagon department you enter the coach-building room, in continuation of which are the repairing shop and smithy attached.*
>
> *The next great wing of the building is devoted to the locomotive departments. It presents the aspects of a Polytechnic Institution: all the vast implements of engineering science seem gathered together here. Planing machines of all forms and sizes fill up the centre, connected with endless straps to a power-transmitting drum; while on either side the lathes, punching, shearing and cutting machines. In the extreme wing is the brass foundry and brass works.*
>
> *Not the least marvellous thing about this extensive establishment was the fact that the power which moved all the machinery throughout the buildings, covering thirty acres, was transmitted from one steam-engine of twenty-horse power, worked on the Cornish or expansive principle. The arrangements secure the most perfect division of labour, and although six hundred men are employed, there was a total absence of bustle, hurry or confusion. Each man like the machinery, seemed to fall naturally into its own place.*

The works benefited greatly from the improvements in machine tools made in the previous half-century which, as the description suggests, were run by overhead line shafts and belts, powered by the steam engine. However, a lot of the work was still manual. Because wrought iron sheets were only available in quite small sizes, large units such as boilers could only be built by riveting several sheets together. The first step would be to bend the metal to the correct shape on a former, the idea being to produce a finished boiler as nearly circular in cross-section as possible. This avoided undue stresses from the heat generated in use. Riveting was a skilled job that required excellent team work. First the plates to be joined had to be drilled with matching holes. The rivets themselves were like round headed bolts but with no screw thread. They would be heated in braziers or small furnaces. The men had to act quickly – the red hot rivet would be pushed through the hole and the rounded end held firmly against the outside of the boiler by the worker's hammer. On the far side, a second man would hammer the end over to create a tight fit. The work was incredibly noisy and many riveters became deaf in later life.

There were other specific parts that required skilled labour. Before 1850 most wheel hubs were forged by hand. The first mention of a lathe specifically designed for turning locomotive wheels was advertised by Nasmyth, Gaskell & Co in 1839 and it was claimed it could be used for turning wheels up to 7 foot in diameter. Other improvements soon followed. The most difficult problem, however, came with the forging of axles. Again the description indicates that the work was little different from that of an ordinary blacksmith, except that the temperature of the hearth could be increased by blowing in air with a powered fan, providing a more powerful draught than would be available with ordinary bellows.

A straight axle would be made by forging wrought-iron bars together to form the shaft. Many early engines, however, were built with the cylinders inside the frame, and the drive to the wheel was made by the connecting rods turning a cranked axle. This was far more difficult to make and was often to cause trouble due to cracks where the joints had to be made. It was one of the problems that Locke was keen to solve. Although he was primarily known as a Civil Engineer, he had begun his apprenticeship at the Stephenson locomotive works at Newcastle. He was very much involved in designing the first locomotives to be built at Crewe. One of his first tasks was to appoint a good man to overlook the locomotive works, and his choice went to William Buddicom.

It is quite surprising to find Buddicom as an engineer, given his family background. His father was a clergyman, who educated his son at home, concentrating on the classics. The boy, however, was far more interested in things mechanical and took an engineering apprenticeship in 1831 with Mather, Dixon & Co. of Liverpool, who began manufacturing locomotives designed by Edward Bury. In 1836 he got a job as Resident Engineer on the Liverpool & Manchester, where his job involved looking after the stationary engines at Edge Hill. It was there that he first met Locke, who later persuaded him to move to a line in Scotland for which he was Chief Engineer, the Glasgow, Paisley, Kilmarnock and Ayr Railway. He took the job and clearly made a good impression on Locke, during his visits to Scotland. In 1839, Locke offered Buddicom the job of locomotive superintendent and was able to write to him on 3 January the following year:

You are now appointed to the locomotive department at a salary of £500 which I hope will be satisfactory to you, and if you don't turn out one of the cleverest fellows that ever ruled a company I have been talking and protesting too much in your favour. I have only one word to say more. I am deeply anxious for its successful administration. You were recently a stranger to me. I have taken a fancy to your zeal and active habit and thus it is that I depend on you for that aid, of which in this department we stand so much in need. We have done our utmost to make the way straight. Many things want doing. I have written a report on the subject, which has been approved, and is to be carried on; and on this I will talk to you personally, and will put you firstly into a fair way, and secondly (and I hope lastly) will aid you by my council.

Buddicom was to be joined by another new recruit, Alexander Allan, who had previously worked for the Vauxhall foundry in Liverpool. Together they set about looking at ways to solve the most urgent problem on Locke's shopping list: broken and cracked crank axles.

As Locke had reported at the time, the great majority of the engines in use on the Grand Junction in the early days had come from the Stephenson works. Locomotive design had come a long way since the days of *Rocket* and its immediate successors. The need for bigger engines meant that it was necessary to support the extra weight, by adding a third trailing axle to give a 2-2-2 configuration. By the early 1840s the predominant models of this type were the Patentees, engines that also had improved valve gear. They were undoubtedly very fine machines, but they did still have the internal cylinders. Buddicom and Allan decided that the only way to remedy the problem of repairs was to change the Patentees, by rearranging the drive mechanism by placing the cylinders outside the frame. This removed the need for cranked axles, as the piston could be attached directly through connecting rods to cranks on the two drive wheels. The success of the scheme encouraged Locke to begin the work of designing locomotives to be built at Crewe.

Locke was certainly heavily involved in the design of the first locomotives from the works. He had already shown his enthusiasm for design as early as 1832, when he had produced plans for a new type of boiler, which had actually been approved by the Stephensons and was said to be better then anything seen before. The new engines became known as the 'Crewe types'. In order to maintain the rigidity and strength of the sandwich frames used by Stephenson, an extra frame was added and the cylinders placed between them. As the new engine began to take shape, Buddicom left Crewe for France, a move that will be described later, and his place was taken by Francis Trevithick, son of the locomotive pioneer. One locomotive of the Crewe type has survived, built at the works in 1845. It was named *Columbine* and has been preserved at the National Railway Museum in York. There were to be other differences introduced, including a slight modification of the Stephenson valve gear devised by Allan. It was the start of a highly successful engine construction business.

One of the secrets of their success was that they did not indulge in tinkering with successful designs. Locke, in his report of 1839, wrote of 'the folly and expense of perpetually altering the engines for the sake of some trifling gain.' By not making too many alterations it became a simple matter to standardise parts. This seems obvious now, but it seems was not generally practiced. Trevithick later wrote, 'I lately found an engine standing idle for the want of a valve to the pump, a small piece of brass not more than 3lb. in weight, and although there are ten engines of the same class on the line (with two pumps to each engines), there was not one duplicate valve on the establishment.' All that was changed, and Crewe engines developed a high reputation for reliability.

Crewe was a vital addition to the Grand Junction and its later associated lines, a fact that was obvious by the grand celebrations that marked its official opening in December 1843. There was a grand dinner, with all the usual speeches and toasts, including one specifically thanking Locke for his work in making it all possible. It was followed by a ball:

Although there might be at times upwards of 1,500 persons present, there was ample space for all throughout the whole evening.

Several Directors and their families joined in the merry dance; and the Highland bagpipes finished off with The Campbells are Coming and played in front of the assemblage when they retired. While the dance was going on the villagers and neighbours were entertained with a splendid exhibition of fireworks, provided at the expense of the Railway Company. Altogether this was a joyful day.

While Crewe was being developed as a major centre for construction and repair, Locke was soon having to turn his attention to matters further from home.

Chapter Nine
RAILWAYS IN FRANCE

There had been a modest beginning to railway construction in France. The first route between St Etienne and Andrézieux was opened in 1823 for freight only and was followed by the line from St Etienne to Lyons, France's first passenger line. It was for this route that Seguin designed his multi-tubular boiler locomotive at much the same time as Robert Stephenson introduced a similar type in *Rocket*. But then nothing much happened for some time, apart from a couple of short lines opened between Paris and Versailles and St Germain.

The construction of the London & Southampton Railway brought out new plans for a cross-channel link from the rapidly developing port of Southampton. The optimistically named London & Paris Railway was actively promoted by British investors and Charles Vignoles was invited to survey a possible route. The obvious route for the shortest sea crossing to France was to Calais and across to Dover, but not to Southampton: that was ruled out. An alternative from Paris to Dieppe with a branch to Rouen was proposed for France instead. The survey was carried out in 1833 and the French Minister of Public Institutions, Monsieur Thiers, visited England to see for himself the effect of railways in that country. Far from being enthralled, he was aghast, regarded railways as monstrosities and declared he would never allow any further construction in France. Not everyone shared his views and the banker Charles Lafitte was particularly horrified at the Minister's failure to understand the economic consequences of not creating a rail network. He was equally scornful of other sections of society who stood in the way of the transport revolution, railing against 'the dearth of capital, the mistrust of the inhabitants, the charlatanism of speculators.'

Lafitte decided to try and move the situation forward and recruited an English entrepreneur, Edward Blount, who was well qualified for the task. Born in 1809, he began his working life in banking, but by 1829 he had moved into the world of diplomacy, as attaché to Lord Granville at the Paris Embassy, where he made many valuable connections including the future Napoleon III. He then decided that diplomacy was not the life for him, and as he had a private income was able to dabble in journalism, becoming a regular correspondent for the world's first railway newspaper *The Railway Chronicle*. With good connections, railway knowledge and enthusiasm he at once accepted the invitation to form a company, Lafitte, Blount & Cie, to promote railway construction in France.

They approached the London & Southampton Railway to gain their support for a new line to Le Havre. This was so obviously in the former's interest that they promptly backed the proposal that now had to go to the French government. It was equally obvious that the man for the post of Chief Engineer would be Joseph Locke. We are fortunate in having a very full account of Locke's involvement in the project as he made it the subject of his inaugural address when he was appointed President of the Institution of Civil Engineers and the entire speech was printed in the Institution's reports for 1857-8. As Locke remarked at the beginning of the speech, there was not much point in talking about railway engineering in Britain, a subject with which most of the audience would have been very familiar, but he thought they might be interested in knowing how things were done in France.

The main difference was the government involvement in the whole process. The ideas were submitted to the Administration of the Ponts et Chaussées department who decide which routes were appropriate 'for the public utility'. Once plans had been approved they were handed to the Minister of Public Works, who then passed on the information to the local communes along the proposed route: 'the Mayor announces, by an advertisement on the doors of the Marie and by a beat of drum, that the plans have been received; and that they are ready for inspection by any parties whose land may be affected.' Any objections were considered and dealt with and then the process of land purchase began, negotiating prices by mutual agreement. After that the land became the property of the Company for a fixed length of time.

Locke approved the French system, particularly the fact that the system only allowed lines that were shown to be essential improvements on anything already in place. It removed the Parliamentary battles that were a feature of the British system, and which led to 'the encouragement of a rivalry that leads to contention and unprofitable works.' It also avoided the rivalries between different companies that had 'duplicated, nay trebled, both lines and stations.' He ended this part of his speech by noting: 'the railway interest in France has not, as in England, been made a victim of public exigencies and private cupidity.'

Locke was duly appointed as Chief Engineer in France. It was decided that work should be limited at first to the Paris-Rouen line, as the engineering would be far simpler than on the extension to Le Havre. In his report on the line he wrote:

The country is only slightly irregular; the embankments will be light. The heaviest works will be three tunnels and four bridges. The longest tunnel will be a mile and a half in length, but it will be through an excellent material, for the soil is chalk. The bridges will not cost more than £15,000 each. They will be made of wood, with a span of about 100 feet, and have four arches. The French are peculiar for making works of this kind last as long as iron.

He hoped to finish the whole line at a very reasonable price of around £20,000 a mile, by using cheap French labour. 'When I became Engineer to the Paris and Rouen Railway, I of course very soon turned my attention to the means which that country offered for enabling me to construct and maintain my works.' He soon discovered that the country offered very little. Contractors put in extravagant estimates, which were totally unrealistic. He turned instead to the contractors that he trusted the most: Thomas Brassey and William Mackenzie. At first they put in separate bids, but then agreed to combine their forces and take the whole contract. Mackenzie noted in his diary in July 1840 that he and his wife had met with Mr and Mrs Locke to talk about the Rouen Railway during work on the Glasgow, Paisley & Greenock line – one of the first indications that Phoebe joined her husband on his travels. It all sounds very good natured, but friendship did not stop Locke striking a hard bargain when it came to contracts. He made his estimates of costs with scrupulous care and was seldom prepared to bargain, as Mackenzie found out at another meeting in Scotland that December. Locke proposed a price of £40 a yard for the work but Mackenzie had asked for £42. Mackenzie then suggested a compromise at £41 but Locke was having none of it, so reluctantly Mackenzie agreed to the lower price. Brassey was annoyed and felt that Mackenzie had given in too easily.

If Locke was unhappy with French contractors, he was equally disappointed with the French workers, who had no experience of navvying, nor even of the tools and equipment regularly in use in Britain. He explained the situation when Mackenzie and Brassey arrived in France, bringing their army of navvies with them:

Among the appliances carried by these gentlemen, there were none more striking or important then the navvies themselves. Following in the wake of their masters, when it was known that they had contracted for works in France, these men soon spread over Normandy, where they became objects of interest to the community, not only by the peculiarity of their dress, but by their uncouth size, habits, and manners; which formed so marked a contrast with those of the peasantry of that country. These men were generally employed in the most difficult and laborious work, and by that means earned larger wages than the rest of the men. Discarding the wooden shovels and basket-sized barrows of the Frenchmen, they used the tools which modern art had suggested, and which none but the most expert and robust could wield.

The navvies at work were admired as Locke recorded in his address:

I think as fine a spectacle as any man could witness, who is accustomed to look at work, is to see a cutting in full operation, with about twenty wagons being filled, every man at his post and every man with his shirt open, working in the heat of the day, the gangers looking about, and everything going like clockwork. Such an exhibition of physical power attracted many French gentlemen, and looking at these English workmen with astonishment, said, 'Mon Dieu! Les Anglais. Comme ils travaillent.' Another thing that called forth remark, was the complete silence that prevailed amongst the men. It was a fine sight to see the Englishmen that were there, with their muscular arms and hands hairy and brown.

The British navvies were noted for their prowess. It was estimated that in filling wagons a good navvy's work was the equivalent of lifting 20 tons of spoil to a height of six feet in a day's work. The French who started at the work could not match this and, as a result, they received generally two and a half francs a day and the British twice as much. As the pay received by the French was far more than they had managed to earn in their earlier life as farm labourers and the like, they were quite happy at first: they respected the British for their expertise and the local shopkeepers were equally content:

The abundance of five-franc pieces, on the Saturday, at all the shops and places of trade, soon made the distributors of them popular; and it was a remarkable fact, well known at the time, that in tunnelling, or other dangerous work, the French labourers could not be induced to join unless an Englishman was at the head of the operations.

The consequences of the Saturday spending sprees were predictable: the 'places of trade' were generally trading in only one commodity. The men had not, said Locke, lost their 'lawless and dangerous' habits – habits that soon brought out the local gendarmes, 'who, however, soon discovered that it was better to humour for a time rather than attempt to control them.' The navvies may have been hard drinkers, but one reason for their fitness and strength was, Locke said, due to the better diet they enjoyed: 'beef and bacon' was better than the French 'coarse bread and an apple'. It is also understandable that the French wanted the reassurance of experienced men on hand in the tunnels. The work was described as unpleasant and frightening. The air was bad, the men were often soaked to the skin and the noise in the tunnels was not reassuring. 'At times you hear alarming creaking noises round you, the earth threatening to cave in and overwhelm the labourers.'

The British and French were not the only ones at work on site. Arthur Helps, in his book *Life and Labours of Mr. Brassey*, 1872, gives a vivid account of this polyglot community:

But among the navvies there grew up a language which could hardly be said to be either French or English; and which, in fact, must have resembled that strange compound (Pigeon English) which is spoken at Hong Kong by the Chinese ...This composite language had its own forms and grammar; and it seems to have been made use of in other countries besides France; for afterwards there were young Savoyards who became quite skilled in the use of this particular language, and who were employed as cheap interpreters between the sub-contractors and the native workmen ...on this railway between Paris and Rouen there were no fewer than eleven languages spoken on the works. The British spoke English; the Irish, Erse; the Highlanders, Gaelic; and the

Welshmen, Welsh. Then there were French, Germans, Belgians, Dutch, Piedmontese, Spaniards, and Poles – all speaking their own language. There was only one Portuguese.

When the common language failed, the British had their own basic means of communication: 'They pointed to the earth to be moved, or the wagon to be filled, used the word 'd-n' emphatically, stamped their feet, and somehow or other instructions, thus conveyed, were generally comprehended by the foreigner.'

We are fortunate in having accounts of the work from both the main contractors, and from William Mackenzie's brother Edward we have details of the day-to-day activities on the Le Havre and Rouen lines. What becomes clear is the close, if not always amicable, relationship between the engineer and the contractors. For his part, Locke was a great believer in being the man on the spot. This was in contrast to the French engineers, who tended to stay at their desks and leave it to assistants to stomp around in the cold and the damp. Locke disapproved:

The experienced eye, on such occasions, sees more than any pen can describe – and elicits, by enquiries and inspections, much that would never occur from the perusal of a statement in writing...On paper it is highly methodical and imposing – copious documents; all is minutely recorded, and cross referenced ... But this will hardly be deemed an efficient substitute for the less formal, but more direct process, by which the engineer is thrown into constant personal relation to the realities with which he has to deal, attacking them, as we have said, with the full weight of his own proper energies; doing nothing of importance at second- or third-hand, but directly grappling with all that is material to the success of his undertaking.

Locke could not escape the French system altogether. The Ponts et Chaussées appointed their own engineer to look over the works, and directors were also liable to appear on the scene. They received little encouragement: 'I have found it necessary to resist undue encroachment.'

Relations between Mackenzie and Locke were not always cordial. All the early descriptions of Locke seem to suggest a very cheerful, good-humoured personality. Mackenzie, in his diary entries, often presents a rather different aspect of the man. An entry for 31 October 1842 finds the two at Poissy: 'we made little progress. Mr. Locke was all day in a very tyrannical humour and took the most unjust views of all matters that came under his view. We did not settle any one thing.' The following year on another visit to Poissy – 'Locke in an infernal cross humour' and the following year, when trying to settle accounts – 'gave another example of his tyranny and petulance.' However, none of these spats seem to have prevented the two men socialising. In the same month of 1843, when Mackenzie recorded the 'cross humour', he dined with Locke and his wife at the Café du Paris. It was on this occasion that Locke gave the first intimation that he was looking for outlets for his talents outside the world of engineering. He mentioned that he would like to become a Scottish Member of Parliament, though he seems to have made little effort in that direction.

Although Brassey and Mackenzie were the main contractors, and brought their own navvies, local men were also employed. It seems a similar system prevailed to the one used in Britain, where gangers were in charge of the men and collected money from the contractors to pay them. That at least was the theory. One of the French gangers, Lamour, collected the money from Mackenzie and then absconded. Next day the men appeared asking for their wages and were sent packing empty handed. As far as the Mackenzies were concerned, they had paid as agreed and had no intention of paying twice. The third day after the ganger had vanished with the cash, Locke appeared on site with Brassey and discussed the work with Edward Mackenzie, and complained about the quality of the masonry. The party was then supposed to be moving on to the next site, but Lamour's men managed to grab hold of Edward and held on to him for two and a half hours, until a troop of Dragoons turned up to rescue him. Now the law stepped in. The magistrates decided that Mackenzie had indeed met his legal obligation, but in order to keep the peace the men should be paid. Edward was highly disgusted: 'They said this is French law – the people are masters not the magistrates. We had to pay the men 7120 francs – this sum is now to be paid twice.'

History soon repeated itself. Edward had his suspicions about a Belgian ganger called Delmier: 'Returned along the line, paid the Belgian and asked the men if they were satisfied he would pay them. They all said they were. I gave him the money and left them.' The men were wrong. This time, not only were Locke and Brassey again at the works when the trouble broke out, but they had the Minister of Public Works with them as well. But the presence of that august gentleman did nothing to improve the situation: the men were paid in full and Delmier was never seen again.

The line to Rouen had been opened on 3 May 1843, with the usual ceremonials, presided over by two Dukes, in the course of which Locke had been awarded the highly prestigious *Legion d'Honneur*. It meant that work could now begin on the far more difficult route to Le Havre. The first difficulty to overcome was the crossing of the Seine at Rouen with an eight-arched bridge, which, like the bridges on the earlier line, would be a wooden superstructure of eight arches carried on stone piers. There were five tunnels with a total length of 5,500 yards. There were deep cuttings and tall embankments, and a steep drop down to the coast that Locke planned as a line with a gradient of 1 in 110. He was examined before a French committee, whose own engineers declared that the steepest allowable gradient would be 1 in 100. It is a mark of Locke's persuasive powers that the eventual compromise was close to his original estimate – 1 in 125.

The most imposing of all the structures was a viaduct near the town of Barentin, about 12 miles from Rouen. Here it had to cross a valley with a stream at the bottom that powered a number of mills, and a main road. It had 27 arches, each 50 feet span and rising to a maximum height of 100 feet. The foundations were of solid masonry where they could be fixed on solid chalk: elsewhere and by the river, they rested on pilings. The arches themselves were built of bricks, fired on site. The work was almost complete in January 1846 when disaster struck. Devey, in his biography of Locke, gives a vivid account of exactly what happened:

About six o'clock in the morning, as a lad was leading a team of horses up the hill to proceed with the ballasting, he heard bricks falling from the fifth arch on the Rouen side. In a few seconds the arch collapsed; the neighbouring arches followed right and left, rushing to earth with tremendous uproar, until, in two minutes, the whole viaduct fell in, shaking the hills around as if they had been convulsed by a violent earthquake. The mills in the valley were

Attercliffe, Joseph Locke's birthplace as it looked at the early part of the nineteenth century before it was engulfed by Sheffield.

Columbine, the oldest surviving example of a Crewe locomotive built in 1845 and now in the National Railway Museum at York.

Barnsley, where Locke spent most of his childhood, seen here at Queen Victoria's Jubilee, by which time the railway had arrived at the town. (*Barnsley Archives and Local Studies*)

The opening of the Canterbury & Whitstable Railway in 1830, the first line to operate passenger trains with steam locomotives: a lithograph by T.M. Baynes.

The tunnel at Edgehill on the Liverpool & Manchester Railway, a site where Locke worked as assistant engineer under George Stephenson.

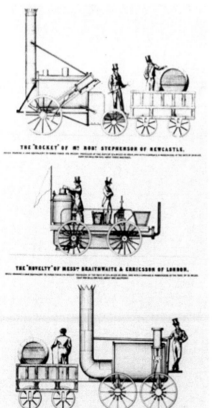

Brusselton incline on the Stockton & Darlington Railway, from Robert Young's biography of Timothy Hackworth, 1923. There was a proposal to use a system like this, using a stationary engine and cable haulage on the L & MR. The argument against was put by Locke with Robert Stephenson.

The contestant in the Rainhill Trial, that was to determine which, if any, locomotives would run the L & MR.

THE "ROCKET" OF MR ROBT STEPHENSON OF NEWCASTLE.

THE "NOVELTY" OF MESSRS BRAITHWAITE & ERRICSSON OF LONDON.

THE "SANSPAREIL" OF MR HACKWORTH OF DARLINGTON.

Passengers wander across the track at Parkside on the L & MR. It was here that Huskisson had his fatal accident on the opening day.

The contractor Thomas Brassey, who was to become Locke's most trusted associate and friend, from Arthur Helps, *Life and Labours of Mr. Brassey* 1872.

A train for Southampton running through Clapham cutting c.1840, headed by a Sharpie 2-2-2 locomotive, with a train of period stock. (*John Scott Morgan*)

The terminal buildings at Southampton, designed by William Tite, photographed in 1910: the building is now a pub restaurant. (*John Scott Morgan*)

Woodhead tunnels on the Sheffield & Manchester Railway. The two original single-bore tunnels can be seen to the left of the photograph, while a new double tunnel is under construction on the right. An engine house from the earlier construction period can be seen on the horizon. (*Ben Brookshank*)

The engine erection shop at Crewe. (*Science and Society*)

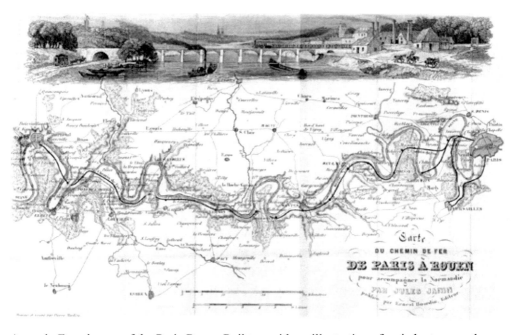

An early French map of the Paris-Rouen Railway with an illustration of a viaduct across the Seine.

Barentin viaduct, which failed catastrophically and had to be entirely rebuilt.

St. Pierre built by Allcard, Buddicom & Cie for the Paris-Rouen Railway in 1845 and now preserved at the Cité du train, Mulhouse. (*Cité du Train*)

The official opening
of the line from Paris
top Le Havre included
the blessing of the
locomotive.

Bishopston cutting on
the Glasgow, Paisley
& Greenock Railway:
it seems probable
that the gentleman
overseeing their works
and wearing a top hat is
the contractor William
Mackenzie. (*University
of Glasgow*)

The London to Glasgow train, double headed with 42319 and 4550 at Low Gill in the wild Cumbrian fells. (*Paul Claxton*)

The original bridge carrying the Richmond, Windsor & Staines Railway across the Thames at Richmond, an engraving from the *Illustrated London News*.

The Windsor line here seen near Datchet c.1840.

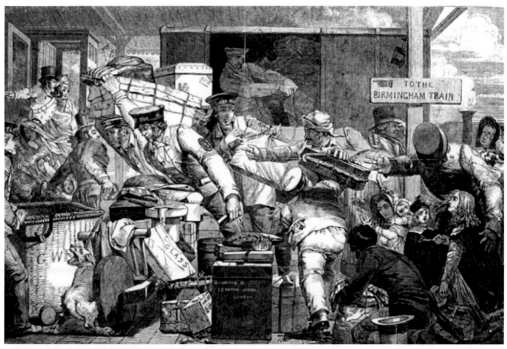

A cartoon depicting the chaos caused by the break of gauge at Gloucester as passengers rush to change from broad gauge to standard gauge.

A replica of *Mataró*: the original, the first locomotive to run in Spain, was built for the Barcelona and Mataró railway. The replica is in the railway museum at Vilanova.

The Bróval tunnel in which Locke had a serious accident during its construction.

Le Gare Montparnasse, the Paris terminus for the Compagnie de l'Ouest.

Buchanan Street station, the original Glasgow terminus of the Caledonian railway was only intended to be a temporary structure but survived into the twentieth century.

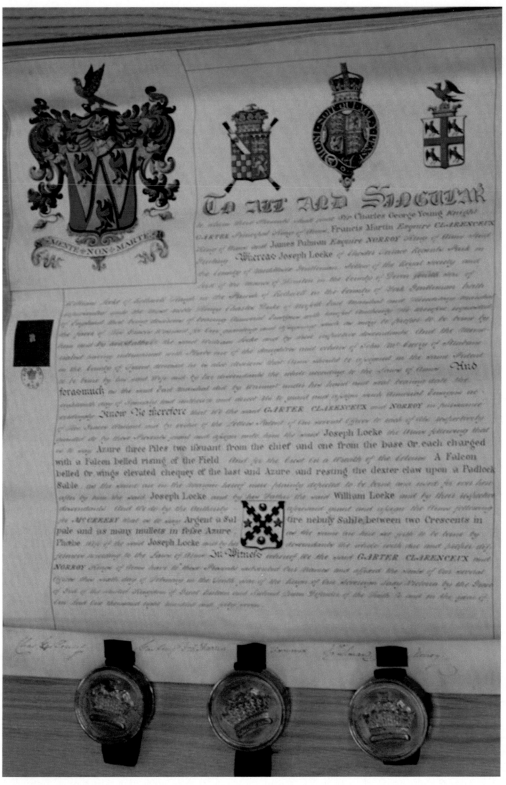

The official document from the College of Heralds awarding Locke his coat of arms.

Robert Stephenson

Robert Stephenson, Locke's old friend and engineering rival, photographed in 1856.

Barnsley Grammar School, endowed by Locke, photographed in 1905. (*Barnsley Archives and Local Studies*)

Joseph Locke's statue in the park named after him in Barnsley.

shattered to pieces, though two or three men buried in the rubble managed to crawl out unhurt.

Devey gives one version of what had gone wrong. He wrote that the disaster had been caused by laying heavy ballast on the top of the viaduct before the mortar had completely set and the arches had been stabilised. He claimed that the Resident Engineer had warned this could happen, and it had been planned to remove the ballast that day. Mackenzie tells a different story in his diary entries:

12 January Mr Illidge informed me on Saturday last Barentin Viaduct fell to the ground a heap of ruins – fault – Bad Mortar. We told Mr Locke mortar was bad and proposed to use Hydraulic for mortar and bear half the expense of the extra. He said he would allow nothing, but we were at liberty to use it if we pleased. The result is now to be seen.

This would be characteristic of Locke's attitude. A price had been agreed and the price was to be kept, but without knowing the original specifications it is difficult to see who is to blame. Mackenzie continues the story:

13 January Today I met Locke with Mr Brassey. He looked sad and was low in spirit. Afterwards went to Newman's office where I found him engaged in making a plan for reconstructing Barentin viaduct and instead of building as before hollow piers opening with 4 chimneys 2'6 " square is now to be solid and the piers instead of brick arches they propose timber ones.

According to Devey the French press 'Set up a howl' blaming their government for employing the British and the British for wretched workmanship. Brassey confounded the critics. With no fuss whatsoever, he announced that he would be rebuilding the viaduct at his own expense. He had undertaken to complete the work and maintain it for twelve months and he would abide by the terms of his contract. It was a huge expense for Brassey, but an enormous boost to his reputation for scrupulous honesty that was to stand him in good stead for the remainder of his career.

Mackenzie and Brassey now began to worry about the other viaduct at Malaunay. Once there they discovered 'some very ugly cracks in the piers that is a little alarming.' They had the piers strengthened and declared themselves satisfied. The French, however, were taking no chances. Before they allowed passenger trains across they first loaded 3,000 tons of earth on top and left it there for several days. Still worried about safety, they brought out a goods train with heavily loaded wagons and ran that backwards and forward a few times. Only when no further cracks appeared did they finally decide it was acceptable.

Brassey completed the building of the Barentin viaduct at a total cost of £20,000, but he did get some relief. He was awarded the £10,000 premium that had been promised by the Company if the line was finished ahead of time. The Rouen & Havre section was officially opened to the public on 22 March 1847. Apart from the usual celebrations, the directors marked the occasion by handing out 12,000 francs to be distributed among the poor in the regions through which the railway passed. At the celebratory dinner, at which Locke was thanked and praised, the engineer did make the point that it could all have been finished a great deal quicker without the tests insisted on by the French engineers. It seems less than gracious, given the justifiable nervousness following the disastrous collapse at Barentin. Even if engineers could have been satisfied, it was probably intended as much to appease the public, as it was to be an actual scientific experiment.

The opening did not mark the end of Locke's involvement with the lines. In his Presidential address he wrote:

I found too that France had then only two or three places where a small number of locomotives engines had ever been made, the rest being obtained from England: and all these at that time, were of a very inferior description. Knowing that the railway system there was then just starting and that France could not, and ought not, to remain without the means of repairing and consequently, of constructing its own engines, I at once determined on the establishing workshops at Rouen: by which that Company at least might be able to rely on resources entirely under its own control.

The works, known as Les Chartreux after a nearby monastery, were established at Sotteville, near Rouen, and Locke brought William Buddicom over from England to run the works, with his partner William Allcard. The three men had all followed similar paths: Allcard had, like Locke, worked under George Stephenson on the Liverpool &

Manchester Railway. The two new men had formed their own company, Allcard, Buddicom & Co. Inevitably, Buddicom drew heavily on his experience at Crewe when designing locomotives for the French railways. There were two types of locomotive produced in the early years: a 2-2-2 for express passenger trains and a 2-4-0 for goods. One of the engines built there in the early days has survived and is now on show at the Cité du Train Museum at Mulhouse in France. The locomotive, *St. Pierre*, is remarkably similar to the Crewe engines. This is one of the 2-2-2 passenger locomotives with 5ft 7½in drive wheels and angled outside cylinders set within a double frame. It has the Allan valve gear as well. It was built between 1843 and 1845 and proved a remarkably successful engine that remained in service right up to 1916 – at the start of the twentieth century it had covered over 800,000 miles in service. It is no wonder that Locke, in his review of French railways, expressed his pleasure at what Buddicom had achieved:

> *The success of this experiment has been complete, both to the company and to Mr. Buddicom, who still continues his labours, and in a much wider field, for he now supplies engines and carriages to most of the companies in France, and I think I may add, that no company, even at the present day, possesses a* matériel *better adapted for railway service, than that which has emanated from the workshops at Rouen.*

So what we think of as the Crewe-type locomotive became known in France as Le Buddicom. Locke's success in France in engineering an important part of the country's new transport system and establishing a major engineering works for locomotives and rolling stock is still remembered in that country. In 1951 a statue of Locke, copied from an original designed by Louis Dubec for Barnsley in 1866, was erected in Barentin in the shadow of the famous – or infamous - viaduct. Locke now left France to face new challenges at home.

Chapter Ten

RAILS NORTH

One of the problems of writing a neat, chronological biography of any engineer is that projects usually overlap instead of following each other in neat succession. The engineer is unlikely to be working on just one line at a time, and this was certainly true of Locke. There was a brief mention in the last chapter of negotiations about French railways taking place in Scotland, where he was Chief Engineer for the Glasgow, Paisley & Greenock Railway. It is now time to backtrack and look at that line in more detail.

The story really begins with the history of the Clyde. Today, we think of it as a mighty river, famous for its ship-building industry, which saw the launch of such celebrated vessels as the *Queen Mary*. Yet at the beginning of the eighteenth century, the river in Glasgow was so shallow that many of its citizens used to ride across on horseback rather than pay the toll to use the bridge. Improvements were put in place in the latter part of that century, but it was still impossible for sea-going vessels to reach Glasgow itself. This led to Greenock's development as the main port near the mouth of the river, from where everything had to be transhipped into smaller river craft. There was an attempt to improve matters by the construction of the Glasgow, Paisley & Ardrossan Canal, authorised in 1806. It never even got much beyond Paisley, before work was abandoned. At the start of the railway age, there was a plan to extend the canal by means of a railway, but this would have been very much on the older pattern, involving a great deal of haulage by stationary engines. There were also a number of tramways connecting to the river, mostly built to a 4ft 6in gauge, and for a time it seemed possible that that would become the standard gauge for Scotland, but wiser councils prevailed, and it was agreed to match the lines already well advanced south of the border. As the development of Greenock moved forward, the need for a better connection to Glasgow became ever more pressing.

Two companies were formed: the Glasgow, Paisley & Greenock and the Glasgow, Paisley & Ardrossan. It was at once obvious that Parliament was highly unlikely to authorise two parallel routes, linking the same places, so agreement was reached that the line between Glasgow and Paisley should be built and operated jointly. From Paisley, the line to Ardrossan swung off in a wide arc to the south, while the other line took a more northerly route. Once agreement had been reached the Acts for the two lines were approved, and it was agreed that to make construction simpler, the incomplete canal to Paisley could be filled in. It must rank as one of Britain's least successful and shortest-lived canals. Locke was appointed as Chief Engineer for the line to Greenock and his Resident Engineer was to be the man he had first met while working in Stockport, and who had worked with him on the Grand Junction, John Errington. Born at Hull in 1806, Errington had trained as a surveyor for civil engineering works in Ireland, before moving back to Britain. His work on the Grand Junction had begun in the comparatively lowly position of assistant surveyor, but when Locke took over the whole line he became the Resident Engineer. In 1840 Locke took him into partnership.

As this was a joint enterprise, Locke only took direct responsibility for the first seven miles. The first part of the route presented few difficulties. One of the first problems was bringing the line into Paisley itself, on a multi-arched viaduct, followed by the crossing of the White Cart at Paisley. The Ardrossan line had a ready-made start, adapting the original canal aqueduct, but Locke had to design a new bridge. He decided to build it entirely from stone and to build it to last. The foundations were 8 feet below the stream bed, and the 85-foot single span rose to a height of 54 feet. It was a colossal undertaking that required over 3,000 tons of stone. In order to bring the huge stone blocks from the quarry to the site, Locke arranged for the construction of a temporary railway. The trucks lumbering up to the viaduct site with their massive loads were described by one imaginative local as being like 'a huge land-turtle creeping up a hill with a sheep on its back.' The viaduct was later widened.

Beyond Paisley was the greatest obstacle to progress, a high ridge that lay right across the line at Bishopton. Here deep cuttings had to be carved through hard rock at each side of the ridge, joined by a pair of tunnels, 330 and 352 yards long, thrust out from either side of a huge 65-foot deep shaft. As usual, Locke put the major works out to tender to experienced contractors. Thomas Brassey got work at the Glasgow end, but the Bishopton contract went to William Mackenzie, who put in a final bid at £88,264 - £20,000 lower than Brassey's bid. He was soon to discover that Brassey's estimate was rather more realistic. The work was to prove far more difficult than anyone had expected. Mackenzie himself was busy on many contracts, including those in France, and called on his brother Edward to take over much of the work.

It was not just the terrain that provided problems. In March 1839 he found a subcontractor had been beaten up by his own men, while a month later he arrived at Bishopton before breakfast and discovered all the miners were blind drunk. In his own words: 'I took the work out of their hands, they were very impudent.' One can imagine that 'very impudent' hardly describes what a drunken miner might have said to him.

Every effort was made to finish the work on time. Mackenzie brought in a thousand men at one time and set them working day and night. He had to pay them extra, but they weren't satisfied with the rates of pay, and when a rock fall killed one of the workers, a large proportion of the workforce simply packed their belongings and left. It was, said Locke, 'ruinous to the contractors.' Life could have been made easier if more shafts could have been dug for the tunnel, but the local landowner, Lord Blantyre, refused permission. As it was, the workings were a scene of endless activity and blasting was a regular event, every day for hours on end, each shot preceded by a blast on a bugle to warn people to keep clear. 'The twanging of horns. The grating noise of the iron borers and the heavy and incessant explosions stunning the ear on all sides like the roar of artillery.' The author of those words added that visiting the site was like entering a war zone.

Physical problems were not the only thing that caused difficulties for the Mackenzie brothers. Relations with Locke seem to have been good, but they had far more trouble with Errington. In the summer of 1839 Locke toured the works and declared himself satisfied, but when Errington appeared shortly afterwards, 'he complained of everything he saw, nothing was right.' And as the contractors were pushing on as rapidly as possible, Errington was not always being helpful:

Errington called and went down on the Engine – he pressed the Engine on to Paisley which prevented me from sending out about 50 Waggons, I wish the Directors would keep a special Train and

*Engine for such like Men. I suffer much from such Mens greatness,
his carcase being carried on it seems is of more importance [than]
50 Waggons of Stone going out of the cutting.*

Locke reported back to the directors and explained to them that the
delays in completing the work were not down to incompetence or lack
of effort by the contractors who had done all that was humanly possible.
That did not, however, help when it came to costing the work. When the
cuttings were measured to assess the work involved, Errington's
estimates fell far short of Mackenzie's, who claimed to have lost
something like £10,000. The Glasgow, Paisley & Greenock may have
been a comparatively short line, but it was one beset with difficulties.
For Mackenzie, trying to balance his life with his other interests both at
home and abroad, it often seemed like a nightmare. It was he declared a
'hot shop. If purgatory is to be compared with it, I'll try and avoid it.'
For Locke, it marked the start of a far longer association with Scotland.

The opening of the new lines made visiting Scotland very much easier
than it had been in the past. Travellers from London could go by train
all the way to Liverpool after which they could get a steamer to
Ardrossan, a 14-hour journey, and continue to Glasgow by train. This
does not seem particularly speedy to us, but it was far better than any
stage-coach journey could have been, and even the *Railway Times*
considered it almost ideal. 'What more could any reasonable man want?
If he were to travel the whole way by rail at 20 miles an hour, he could
but arrive two or three hours earlier, before breakfast was ready or
anyone up to bid him welcome.' However, by 1840, the opening of the
Lancaster and Preston Junction Railway now meant that there was a
direct route from London as far north as Lancaster. At some time there
was going to be a connecting rail link between England and Scotland,
and this provided an opportunity to make that connection along the west
coast. But it was not the only contender: there was another line to the
north from London, completed that year, this time joining the capital to
York. It offered the possibility of an east coast line to Edinburgh. No
one, at the time, felt that two routes to Scotland were necessary; one
should be quite sufficient.

Locke had appreciated from the time that he was first appointed as
Chief Engineer to the Grand Junction, that there was always the
possibility that it would form part of a through route to Scotland and in

1836 he published a report setting out his ideas: *The London & Glasgow Railroad through Lancashire.* He had a mental picture of where the line should go, though he had never carried out a proper survey. The first 'official' guide to the railway that was eventually built was written in 1855 by George Measom and it vividly describes the choice faced by the young engineer:

The genius of Joseph Locke showed itself. He grappled with the mountain region of Westmorland, and looked steadily at the summits and valleys which had deterred others. Whether to bend round by Kirkby Lonsdale and Appleby, or to keep more westward by Kendal and Penrith; whether to tunnel under the bleak Shap Fell, or to ascend the passes between its summit by steep inclines, or to avoid it altogether by a detour; whether to make tunnels and viaducts and embankments or steep gradients?

His eventual decision was to opt for the tunnel and Shap Fell. He never, it seems, even contemplated taking a more roundabout route along the coast.

George Stephenson also looked at the possibilities of heading north from Lancaster. He had taken an 'ocular survey' of likely routes, setting off on 1 August 1837. The first part of his journey took him up the east coast, after which he investigated the route that would cross Shap Fell and would follow the Lune Valley. He dismissed the Shap route as impractical in his report written on 16 August:

There is a very serious consideration which has not been sufficiently regarded by companies projecting Railways over high countries, namely, the great length of winters, the quantity of snow falling on high lands, and the length of time it remains upon the ground. These disadvantages coupled with the effect produced by the ice upon the rails, will, in my opinion, be an insurmountable difficulty to the passing of the Shap ridge, especially as the inclinations at the summit must be steep.

His preferred route was along the flat land of the east coast, which would be reached by building a barrage across Morecambe Bay. Although it was longer, he estimated that because of the difficulties of the inland route it would be just as quick, and would be considerably cheaper to build. He concluded, 'I have no hesitation in expressing my decided conviction of the superiority of the Coast line.'

Arguments went backwards and forwards and Stephenson continued to find new objections to the Locke route, including stating that the route was 'attained by pursuing the sinuosities of mountain valleys, where every now and then the direct course is obstructed by obtruding eminences which, after much cutting, still require to be passed round in considerable curves.' He thought that even when travelling at 'mail-coach speed' the train was likely to be derailed. Locke ignored this criticism but did consider some alternatives to his original idea, though still keeping well inland. A third engineer, George Larmer, joined in the fray with yet another alternative, through Orton with a tunnel under Orton Scar. Still nothing much happened, and an exasperated citizen of Kendal, Cornelius Nicholson, who owned a local paper mill decided to make the case for the railway to be brought to his home town, and published a pamphlet to argue the case. The result was a public meeting and the formation of a separate Kendal Committee, who came up with yet two more routes. Someone at some time had to start taking decisions.

The whole question of what was to be the best rail route between England and Scotland was to be decided by a Royal Commission headed by Lt. Col. Sir Frederic Smith and Professor Peter Barley, a mathematician from the Royal Military Academy at Woolwich. They not only had to decide between these competing schemes, but also as it was generally agreed at that time that one line would be quite enough to join the two countries, whether it should be built in the west at all. Stephenson's preferred route was an early casualty, in part because the Admiralty objected to the construction of the barrage across Morecambe Bay. This would have come as no surprise to another engineer. Brunel had little but contempt for that body of men: 'they have an unlimited supply of *some negative* principle which seems to absorb and eliminate everything that approaches them.' Eventually they decided on the western line, but were still uncertain about the route up the Lune valley and suspicious about the practicality of the proposed tunnel. They also suggested that the line could usefully be brought nearer to Kendal, to the delight of Cornelius Nicholson. Unfortunately, by the time they reported, the country was undergoing a financial slump and there were no funds for railway construction of any kind. The different plans were put back on the shelf.

Eventually, a second Commission was appointed, and this time they were happy to agree that there was room for two routes to Scotland, and saw no objection to a line from Newcastle to Edinburgh. This spurred everyone into action. Public meetings were called and there was a new sense of urgency – things had to be agreed so that work could start before the rivals on the east coast established their route over the border and grabbed all the traffic. The agreed route was the one proposed by the Grand Junction with the co-operation of the Lancaster & Preston Junction: Locke's route over Beattock summit, but without any tunnel. Everything finally seemed set for construction to start when new objections appeared. There was opposition from residents of the Lune valley, who didn't want a railway at all, and Lord Lowther raised objections to the route passing through Lowther as it was too close to his magnificent Lowther Castle. Even some Grand Junction shareholders objected to the line, on the grounds that there weren't enough people en route to make it pay 'unless the crows were to contract with the railway people to be conveyed at low fares.' But by the end of 1843 most objections had been withdrawn and the way was open to prepare a Bill for Parliament. It was passed the following year with no real scrutiny – which was just as well as plans had been drawn up so hurriedly that one section had actually been copied from an old county map. Finally work could get under way, but thanks to all the delays the east coast route being pushed ahead under the auspices of the Railway King, George Hudson, already had a substantial lead in the race to Scotland.

There was such an intense sense of urgency in the Lancaster and Carlisle camp that tenders for the construction contract were invited even before the Act had been obtained. In his biography of William Mackenzie (2004), David Brooke describes how the main contractors got together in a spot of price fixing. The cheapest estimate was supplied by John Stephenson, who had previously worked on the Sheffield and Rotherham Railway. The other bids were put in by Brassey and Mackenzie. But before any of them were sent to the Company, they persuaded Stephenson to increase the value of his bid and they would increase theirs, but would be still kept higher than his price. In return, they would receive a 'bonus' of £20,000. It would seem that Brassey and Mackenzie were not too keen on this difficult route, but wanted something out of the process. In the event, the company directors were reluctant to hand the whole contract to Stephenson on his own and persuaded the three of them to combine forces to undertake the work. So everything was now in place, with Locke as Chief Engineer, Errington as Resident Engineer and the newly formed trilogy of contractors to undertake all the construction.

Discussions about the route went on to the very end. Locke's first plans had included a tunnel, but his distaste for tunnelling in general soon led to him considering alternatives. His final route did not please everyone. Among the most vociferous supporters of the line were the citizens of Kendal, but now their nearest station would be 2 miles away at Oxenholme. Instead of a tunnel, the new line would simply go up and over the hills, which would involve first of all a journey down the Lune gorge and a climb up Grayrigg to a height of 600 feet, the last part being a 2-mile run at 1 in 106. This was already an extreme gradient, but it was followed at Tebay by a 4-mile climb up Shap Fell at the unprecedented gradient of 1 in 75. After that effort, the 7-mile run down to Carlisle must have seemed quite modest at 1 in 125. Locke could have suggested that the loss of time involved in puffing up one side would be saved by the high speed created going down, but that would have given many investors an alarming vision of a locomotive and its train dashing out of control down the steepest slope. He had, in fact, carried out experiments on gradients and had discovered that on a 1 in 250 slope, a carriage only just began to move, overcoming air resistance and friction. On any greater slope, a braking system would be essential. Like most engineers of that time, who had learned on the job rather than in the classroom, he relied far more on experiment than on theory. His experiments satisfied him that gradients needed to be taken seriously but that he was confident about safety.

The most likely objection to the proposed route over Shap was the obvious one: the gradient was simply too steep. He put the case that though it was difficult in the present state of locomotive development, a time would come when engines would climb the slope with little problem. He was right in his assumption, but it was not to happen in his lifetime, nor even in his century. His final argument, which probably persuaded the financiers of the Company, was that though it would be costly to run, the extra cost would be more than compensated by the reduced costs of construction. Again, he was right in the short term, but the costs of getting trains up to the Shap summit lasted well beyond the point where they were covered by construction savings. For many decades, banking engines had to be kept at Tebay to help in the long haul up the slope: a tedious job for the crews, who spent their days going up and down the same stretch of line over and over again.

The first sod was cut in the summer of 1844, just a month after the passing of the Act and, by the end of the year, it was reported that 3,761 men were employed on the line, while 387 horses had been set to work moving spoil and bringing material to the sites. By then work was going on at seventy-five different sites along the whole route. It was only after work was well under way that the Company revised their original short-sighted decision to build the line as a single track, which would have had a disastrous effect on running an efficient service, and opted for a more conventional double track. This necessarily involved extra work and extra costs, especially on the most difficult work at Shap. The cutting there had to be blasted out of what was described as hard whinstone rock, something of a tautology, as 'whinstone' simply means hard rock and the name comes from the noise it makes when hit with a hammer. In fact they had to make their way through one of the hardest of all rocks, granite.

The cutting was a quarter of a mile long and sixty feet deep and involved the removal of 350,000 cubic yards of material. Five hundred men worked at Shap for two years and used 23 tons of gunpowder to blast their way through. A contemporary guide was probably an accurate representation of the attitude towards the navvies who carried out the dangerous work:

Few lives were sacrificed during the progress of this great work, considering the number of men engaged here, the length of time, and their kind of employment; and more especially their miserably deficient state of education, which when liberally given assists materially towards making more skilful workmen and better subjects.

The implication is that the men were too ill-educated to look after themselves properly and take care of their own safety. There was no suggestion that their employers might take some of that responsibility on their behalf. It was not that the contractors were bad employers by the standards of the time: it was generally accepted that accidents were unavoidable and probably the fault of the men involved. It is difficult to judge how the death rates compared on different lines, since accurate records were seldom kept. In fact Stephenson, Brassey and Mackenzie did far more for their navvies than many other contractors did at that time.

It is hard now to realise just how remote and wild this region was at the time. Today the railway is overshadowed by the M6 and cars zoom along with no awareness of gradients or problems. But then it was inhospitable and only thinly populated, though there was a scheme to turn Shap into a fashionable spa, hopefully named Shap Wells. It never materialised. To meet the men's needs the contractors built huts with sod walls and thatched roofs, described by the *Railway Record* as offering a standard of comfort 'which surpasses all belief', unlikely as it may sound. They also provided a church and school room. The navvies gave their little settlement names with a nice touch of irony – Regent Street and Hanover Square were two of the thoroughfares lined with their mud hovels.

With so many hard-working, hard-living men crowded together, there were inevitably some hard cases who caused trouble. The neighbourhood where the work was being carried on was plagued by accounts of drunken behaviour, especially after the monthly payday. There were also more serious claims of theft and even rape. There was little the authorities could do. There were few police – no more than eight special constables on the whole line. When a fight broke out between eight navvies, the local constable refused to arrest them on the very reasonable grounds that he didn't have a gaol to put them in. The most serious problems occurred due to rivalries between the different groups at work – English, Scots and Irish. The English, it was said, were happy to join in any fight that was going but the real antagonism was between the Scots and Irish. In part it was the old antagonism between Protestant Scots and Catholic Irish, but there was a more mundane cause of hostility. The Irish were accused of working for lower wages. There were frequent skirmishes and the contractors did their best to keep the three groups apart. But the biggest trouble of all began with a minor incident.

At workings near Penrith an English ganger ordered an Irishman to stop working with a pickaxe and start using a shovel. He refused and the Irish on the site were told to leave. The next day, the Irish returned in force: an estimated 500 turned up armed with picks and shovels and the English wisely disappeared. The Irish returned to Penrith and the word came that 2,000 English navvies were about to attack them. This time it was the Irish who were outnumbered. Most of them fled the scene, but a few tried to remain in hiding in Penrith. A dozen of the Irish were found in a lodging house and brutally attacked: 'It was a regular butchery, and could be compared with nothing else than turning rats into a box and as many laying on with sticks as could get near them.' One of the most violent ringleaders, John Hobday, was arrested and sentenced to fifteen years transportation.

A select committee was set up by Parliament to enquire into the conditions of the navvies, but was largely concerned with their moral welfare. Among those giving evidence was the Rev. William St George Sargent who had been appointed by a benefactor to act as chaplain to the navvies, but scarcely had a good word to say about them. His main complaints appear to have been that they didn't know their Bibles and were likely to be living with women without the benefit of an official marriage, all of which was probably true. It is easy to get a picture of them, as indeed they were described in the report of 1846, as 'degraded brutes' living 'like savages'. But it is as well to remember that while the local press recorded every misdemeanour, no one was interested in reading accounts that simply said – thousands of men at work, getting on with the job peacefully and quietly. There were troubles, but others took a very different view of the men. A reporter from the *Railway Record* wrote: 'I never saw so great a number of the finest and stoutest workmen together. They are the admiration of all.' They were the men who had the strength and the skills to turn Locke's grand plans into physical reality.

What is indisputable is that the work was carried out with extraordinary speed. By 1846 in the dash to beat the eastern route, the workforce had grown to almost 10,000 and work was going on day and night. By 5 November the directors were able to make the 70-mile journey from Lancaster to Carlisle and on 15 December the line was officially opened with all the usual ceremonies. It had been a triumph for Locke who had planned the route, Errington, the man on the ground, the three contractors and for the thousands of men from navvies to skilled carpenters and masons who had made it all possible. At the heart of this success, however, was Locke's planning. One can have an army of workers but unless it has been made crystal clear as to exactly what they are supposed to do, the result is as liable to be confusion as progress. The engineer had not only drawn up his plans with care, but had ensured that everything was clearly explained to the contractors with carefully written instructions and specifications. Everyone knew what was required and Locke and Errington made sure between them that the instructions were fully and correctly followed. It also helped that the engineers were not having to deal with several small contractors but with a consortium of proven talents and experience.

The emphasis has inevitably been on the Shap cutting and climb, but there were other immense structures to be completed along the way. One of the first, on leaving Lancaster was the viaduct across the Lune, which was originally built with seven stone arches on the south bank and one on the north bank, in between which were three timber spans rising 55 feet above the river. Unusually for a railway viaduct it also had a footbridge, separated from the tracks by railings. It was not destined to last long in that form: most of the timber was soon being replaced, originally with wrought iron. There have been further changes since, and Locke's original viaduct is little more than a memory. The next major obstacle was the deep cutting on the approach to Carnforth. The station achieved fame in the twentieth century as the setting for the movie *Brief Encounter*. The refreshment room where Trevor Howard and Celia Johnson met has now been restored to look just as it did on film and has become a heritage centre.

Now the line enters the bleak hilly country, and there will be more viaducts along the way, of which the grandest is the Lowther, built of locally quarried red sandstone. The six arches take it across the river and also over the approach drive to Lowther Castle. It is a mark of the huge amount of material that had to be shifted during construction of the line that a temporary wooden bridge was built so that material from the cutting on one side of the river could be moved on wagons to build up the approach embankment on the other. Once it was opened for passengers and freight, the service was run by the typical Crewe engines already in use on the Grand Junction. The 2-2-2 passenger locomotives could never have managed Shap unaided, and one can only presume there were banking engines in place from the first or that trains regularly ran double- or even triple-headed. But the line was run successfully, that much we do know even if we don't know any of the operational details, and it showed a healthy profit. Everyone was satisfied – apart from the citizens of Kendal, forced to trudge over to Oxenholme to catch a train.

Cornelius Nicholson, who had led the campaign for the line to Carlisle, was not prepared to accept second best for his home town of Kendal. He began a new campaign for a branch line that would leave the main line at Oxenholme to pass through Kendal and on to Ambleside at the northern end of Lake Windermere and possibly even further into the heart of the Lake District. He can hardly have been surprised that the area's most famous resident took a very different view. William Wordsworth and his sister Dorothy lived just a couple of miles from Ambleside and they had already said that they would have to leave their beloved home at Rydal Mount every summer to avoid the crowds that would appear if the railway was built even as far as Lancaster, though there is no evidence that they did so when that line was completed. This, however, was far worse. The local paper published the proposal for the railway in August 1844, and in October Wordsworth wrote a sonnet *On the Projected Kendal and Windermere Railway*. The first few lines give the flavour of the whole:

> *Is there no nook of English ground secure*
> *From rash assault? Schemes of retirement sown*
> *In youth, and 'mid the busy world kept pure*
> *As when the earliest flowers of hope were blown,*
> *Must perish; how can this blight endure?*

It is not perhaps the pithiest argument against the railways, nor indeed one of Wordsworth's better poems, but the main thrust is clear. A railway would destroy the peace and tranquillity of a beautiful region. On 15 October 1844, the day after the poem was first written, Wordsworth also wrote to Gladstone, who was then President of the Board of Trade:

My Dear Mr. Gladstone

We are in this neighbourhood all in consternation, that is every man of taste and feeling, at the stir which is made for carrying a branch

Railway from Kendal to the head of Windermere. When the subject comes before you officially, as I suppose it will, pray give it more attention than its apparent importance may call for. In fact, the project if carried into effect will destroy the staple *of the Country which is its beauty, and, on the Lord's Day particularly, will prove subversive to its quiet, and be highly injurious to its morals. At present I shall say no more, only let me beg of you to cast your eye over a letter which I propose shortly to address thro' the public Press to our two county members upon this occasion.*
Believe me my dear Mr. Gladstone

Faithfully yours much obliged

Wm. Wordsworth

In the event, the proposal that was brought forward was for a line that would stop short of Ambleside at a point roughly halfway up the lake at what is now the town of Windermere. The directors put the change down to the need to reduce the costs by avoiding an expensive viaduct at Troutbeck on the way to Ambleside, but it would at least have been some consolation to Wordsworth and his sister that the new terminus was to be 3 miles further away. In spite of the poet's efforts, the Act for the branch line passed through Parliament in 1845 without opposition.

The obvious choice for building the line was the team at work on the Lancaster and Carlisle and Locke was once again appointed Chief Engineer. It was a very straightforward route, roughly taking a curving path round the hills to follow the line of the River Gowan. The opening ceremony on 20 April 1847 must have confirmed all Wordsworth's worst nightmares. First came a train of sixteen carriages full of passengers accompanied by a band, shortly followed by another similar train, this time with eighteen carriages, yet more passengers and another band. Two steam yachts plied the waters of the lake and it was reported that many passengers strolled on towards Grasmere, passing close to the poet's home at Rydal Mount. One interesting point that emerged was that the trains needed three locomotives each, because according to the *Westmoreland Gazette*, the available engines were not 'of a very powerful description'. It does make one wonder how, if three locomotives were necessary for this modest line, trains were coping with nearby Shap.

The branch line was an undoubted success and has continued to be used, having survived the Beeching axe that felled so many branch lines in the twentieth century. It was not a line that taxed Locke's skills and expertise in planning and executing the route, but it can still be described as it was over a century ago by Cornelius Nicholson – 'a gem of a line'.

Allthough the major works that occupied Locke in the 1840s were in France and northern Britain, these were by no means the only projects in which he and John Errington, in their newly formed partnership, were involved. Locke was very much in demand, largely thanks to his growing reputation for bringing in lines on time and within budget – and within a budget lower than many other engineers considered feasible.

The existing network was being steadily extended. The Southampton line was the starting point for a London & South Western Railway network. The Windsor, Staines and South Western Railway was not a line that presented many problems, and joined Windsor to Richmond, Surrey. The one major engineering feature was the bridge across the Thames at Richmond. It was an elegant structure of three 100-foot arches, consisting of iron girders supported on stone-faced piers. Given Locke's general preference for stone or brick viaducts, there could be a case for saying that the credit for this one should be given to Errington, but one cannot be sure. It has been altered over the years but it gave good service for many decades before heavier traffic made it necessary to strengthen the structure. Brassey was the contractor for the line.

Locke also worked on another line in the London area, and one with an unusual history. It started with the passing of an Act in 1836 for what was originally known as the Commercial Railway, a line from Blackwall to the Minories district of East London, ending at a site now occupied by Tower Gateway Station on the Docklands Light Railway close to the Tower of London. The original plans were drawn up by John Rennie who decided on the curious gauge of 5ft ½in, but the directors decided at the last minute to change to an engineer with greater railway experience, Robert Stephenson. The line was little more than 3 miles long and Stephenson decided to work it by cable haulage and stationary steam engines. He retained the odd Rennie gauge. It made some sense as there was always a possibility of linking the line into the planned Eastern Counties Railway that was being constructed under the management of the engineer John Braithwaite. The directors of that line had originally suggested building it to Brunel's broad gauge, but Braithwaite persuaded them to opt for 5ft, thus achieving the worst of both worlds. With the opening of the London end of the Eastern Counties Railway, it was decided to extend the line to make a junction at Fenchurch Street. This modest task was given to Locke, while at the same time the original line was converted to the more conventional Stephenson gauge and London Docks were now to be served by a railway that would run locomotives. It was not the most prestigious work that Locke carried out, but it did have an important role to play in the development of the London dockland. Locke also worked on minor lines from Royston to Hitchin with an extension to Shepreth, south of Cambridge.

The original aim of the Eastern Counties had been to build a line from London to Ipswich via Colchester and then continue at a later date to Great Yarmouth. However, they rapidly ran out of funds and work spluttered to a stop. At this point the engineer Peter Bruff stepped in with an alternative plan, for a revised route from Colchester to Ipswich and a new Company was formed, the Eastern Union Railway. Bruff's name rarely crops up in railway history – he is probably better known for founding the seaside resort of Clacton-on-Sea, but it was his initiative that got the work under way and his plans that were approved by Parliament. Locke was called in to be Chief Engineer for the construction period, with Brassey yet again as the contractor.

The opening of the line was quite a grand affair, with a dinner attended by some 200 guests who enjoyed a speech by George Hudson, who lavished praise on Locke. The engineer modestly, and very properly, insisted that much of the credit lay with Peter Bruff, who had rescued the moribund scheme to bring rails to East Anglia. The line certainly bore many of the characteristics we now associate with Locke. The 17-mile line was completed at a cost of £300,000, well below the original estimate and at a cost of slightly less than £20,000 per mile. Among the major engineering features was a double viaduct carrying the lines across two branches of the River Stour, built like many of Locke's bridges at this period from timber. He also engineered the longer route between Haughley and Norwich, a line that presented few engineering problems. It must have come as something of a relief to be dealing with the flat lands of East Anglia instead of trying to force a route through the Cumbrian hills.

Locke, by now, had such a high reputation that other engineers were willing to go to him for an opinion on their own work. Charles Vignoles had put forward a proposal for a line to Dover, the North Kent Railway. He took the plans to Locke who approved them and they were duly submitted to Parliament, but there they met opposition led by Robert Stephenson and were rejected. Locke and Vignoles tried to revive the idea in 1845 but to no avail. Relations between Locke and Stephenson had been soured after the disagreements over the Grand Junction, and this episode probably did little to improve them. Everything, however, was to change two years later.

Robert Stephenson was Chief Engineer for the very important Chester & Holyhead Railway, which was used to carry the mail for the ferry to and from Ireland. His major problem was the crossing of the Menai Straits, but first the River Dee had to be bridged near Chester. It must have seemed a very straightforward affair at first and he had originally planned for a five-arch conventional viaduct in brick or stone. However, he had doubts about the foundations so he decided instead to have a 98ft span made of composite cast-iron girders and wrought-iron trusses. He had already built something similar, though not with quite such a wide span, and so had complete confidence in the design. As soon as the Chester end of the route was opened, trains began to use the line, but on 24 May 1847 three girders snapped under a passing train. The driver later remembered being aware of a strange vibration as he crossed the bridge, and the locomotive had just reached the far side when the collapse occurred. Four people died, including the fireman who was on the tender at the time, and sixteen were injured. It was obvious that there would be an inquest and an official enquiry. If it had found that the accident had been caused by faulty design, then Stephenson's career could have been over. Local opinion ran so high on the subject that there was even talk of charging him with manslaughter.

L.T.C.Rolt, in his biography of George and Robert Stephenson (1960), gives a detailed analysis of the problems inherent in the bridge, which was built with three spans using a combination of long cast-iron I-section girders with wrought-iron truss rods. The cast iron had cracked under compression, but the enquiry was told that the accident must have been caused by the derailment of the train, caused by a broken wheel, which had led to the girder being dealt a heavy blow. Stephenson had, at first, been ready to accept full responsibility for the accident, but the Company persuaded him to go along with this version of the story in order to protect both his own and corporate reputation. An array of engineers, including Brunel and Vignoles, came forward to testify on the engineer's behalf. Locke was well known to have always distrusted cast-iron bridges but he still joined in the defence. There was only one voice raised against him, that of Robertson, engineer of the Chester & Shrewsbury Railway, who argued that the fault was entirely due to bad design, and that the way the wrought-iron trusses were used, far from strengthening the bridge actually caused additional stresses to the girders. Faced with such a wealth of expert evidence on one side, offered by the most respected engineers in the land, with just one comparatively unknown expert offering a different view, the inquest jury could only reach one verdict: accidental death. Rolt is quite clear in his own final verdict: Robertson was right and the great and good were wrong.

Stephenson was particularly grateful to Locke, since relations between them had not been good for some time. Earlier he had been asked to act as a consultant on the French routes for which Locke was responsible and had declined, explaining his reasons that went back to the disagreement with his father:

You are very likely aware that there is an unfriendly feeling between ourselves and Mr. Locke. We think he has used us ill; whether we are right or wrong is not the point. But, under that impression I feel it due to myself to avoid giving him any possible ground for complaint against me.

But Stephenson was well aware that Locke had severe misgivings about the suitability of cast-iron for railway bridges, and could well have turned up at the inquest and said so. Instead he had rallied to the support of his former friend. It brought about a real reconciliation.

Much later in his life, Stephenson wrote his own verdict on cast and wrought-iron composite girders, with only a hint of an excuse for why he had used that system at the Dee crossing:

The objection to this girder is common to all girders in which two independent systems are attempted to be blended; and, as a general principle, all such arrangements should be avoided.

It is useless to say any more on the subject of this form of girder, as since the adoption of wrought iron for girders they have been entirely superseded; they were designed when no other means existed of obtaining iron girders of great span, and the melancholy accident which occurred at Chester is the only existing instance of their failure.

Stephenson's reputation had been saved, but he still faced the far greater challenge in completing the route to Holyhead of how to cross the Menai Straits. The only bridge across at that time was Thomas Telford's suspension bridge, but that type of structure was rightly considered as inappropriate for the heavy traffic of a railway bridge: when first tested the road bridge was seen to sway alarmingly under just the weight of a coach and horses and had required further strengthening. Stephenson needed to find a new, radical solution and he famously came up with the box-girder bridge, in which the trains actually ran inside the oblong, wrought-iron tubes. After the Dee disaster, he was understandably nervous: 'I stood on the verge of a responsibility from which, I confess, I had nearly shrunk.' He looked for reassurance to an old friend, Isambard Brunel, but he also sent the plans to Locke to seek his approval. The reconciliation was complete and, encouraged by his contemporaries, Stephenson went on to complete one of his greatest engineering triumphs, the Britannia Bridge at Menai. He was to go on to use a similar design for an even greater challenge, crossing the St Lawrence River in Canada.

During the 1840s Locke was more than once called on for his expert opinion. For example, in 1843 he was a witness in an enquiry into the deterioration of rails on the London & North Western Railway at which he, naturally enough, recommended double-headed rails of the type he had developed and of appropriate weight. But by far the most important investigation at which he was invited to offer his opinion concerning the great debate about the gauge, with supporters of Brunel's 7ft gauge ranged against Stephenson's 4ft 8½ in gauge.

Brunel's broad-gauge empire had spread steadily since the construction of the first line between London and Bristol. Problems first occurred when there was a head-on meeting at Gloucester – broad gauge arriving from the south, and the Stephenson gauge arriving from Birmingham. As a result, everyone and everything had to change at Gloucester. This was not necessarily a real problem for passengers: even today, living as I do on the line from London through Gloucester to Cheltenham, I still have to change at the latter station to go anywhere further north. But it was a huge inconvenience for freight, involving a great deal of loading and unloading of trucks and wagons. Brunel had a suggestion for overcoming the problem, by having what was in effect a form of containerisation, where goods could be packed into boxes that could be transferred from one gauge vehicle to the other. It was not a new idea: there were early tramways on which the bodies of wagons had been designed so that they could be lifted off their chassis by a crane and dropped directly into the hold of a canal boat at the wharf. But it was not considered seriously for the new railway system. When further breaks in gauge looked likely to take place in the Midlands it was decided enough was enough and a Commission was set up to examine the whole question. The Commissioners were Sir Frederick Smith, former Inspector General of Railways, an obvious choice and two less likely gentlemen, the astronomer George Biddell Airy and a mathematician, Professor Peter Barlow.

Brunel's argument was that the broad gauge allowed faster running than the narrower gauge and suggested a contest to test his claim. After a certain amount of arguing over how and where the contest should be held, it was finally agreed to compare runs on similar tracks with equivalent gradients, between Paddington and Didcot for the Great Western and York to Darlington for the others. Robert Stephenson's latest type of long-boiler locomotive was to bear the colours of their camp, while the somewhat older Firefly class represented the broad gauge. In the event, the GWR engine managed a maximum speed of 60mph against their rival's 53¾mph. But did that prove that broad gauge was better or simply that Gooch's engine had outperformed Stephenson's? In any case we now know that far higher speeds are easily obtainable on the narrower gauge.

Locke, when he came to give his evidence, was sceptical about the whole notion of higher speeds, as he made clear when he was asked whether or not he believed the GWR speeds could be matched on other lines:

In answering that question I may say that I do not exactly know what velocity could be obtained upon the Great Western, not having experience as to that line; but I have no doubt that we could, if it were safe, run our expresses upon either line at 50 m.p.h.; they now travel at 40 m.p.h. Our time to Southampton is two hours and it is 78 miles, very nearly 40 m.p.h. including stoppages, and I am quite sure that if it were a matter of necessity we could travel at 50 m.p.h.

Pressed to say whether he would want to run his trains at the higher speed, he was very definite: 'I am very much opposed to it; I do not think it is safe.' It is rather strange to find the man who had so much confidence in locomotive development that he could assume locomotives would one day cope with the severe gradients over Shap Fell, being so cautious about the idea of safe running at high speeds at some future date.

All these arguments about speed did not really have much to do with the central question: what to do about a break in gauge on the country's railways. If the commission thought it was a major problem, then it was clear that one or other of the versions then in use must be given preference. The question to be decided was – which was it to be? In the event the commission decided that in the future 4ft 8½in should be the standard gauge for Britain's railways. Brunel was disappointed, and it is hard not to sympathise with him. He had, he thought, demonstrated the superiority of his system, and the commissioners had lavished praise on it.

The Commission was very clear in its final report that there should be no expansion of the Great Western system. But when the results were made law by Act of Parliament, it soon became clear that the legislature had been lax in framing the rules, so that Brunel was able to go on building extensive branch lines, based on the system already in place. To Locke this was absurd. He felt that the only answer to the problem was a unified system. As time went on, and nothing changed, he decided to set out the case for standardisation based on the Stephenson gauge. He wrote a pamphlet in the form of a letter to Lord John Russell on 'the best mode of avoiding the evils of mixed-gauge railways.' He put his case bluntly: Parliament had got it wrong:

What a result! England, which has given railways to the world, would see France, Belgium, Germany, Italy and the United States advancing in railway enterprise on a uniform plan – the gauge which England furnished to them; and she would stand alone in the anomalous position of having (because one man of great genius disdained to pursue the path pursued by others, and because Parliament, being careless and indifferent to the subject, allowed one powerful company to deviate from the general plan) engraved on her railway a duplication, a complexity and a ruinous expense, of which I am satisfied it would be spared that could they have been foreseen they would never have been tolerated. Why then My Lord should we pursue a policy which is gradually destroying the capital now invested in railways, and why should we lessen the safety of railway travelling? Why was the Gauge Commission appointed, and why are its warnings disregarded.

Locke was not perhaps being entirely fair to Brunel in saying he 'disdained to follow the path of others.' George Stephenson had never had to think very much about what would be the best gauge for a national network. He had built his first locomotives for older tramways, which were never intended to interconnect and had no function other than to move coal from colliery to river or canal and were originally only intended for horse-drawn wagons not locomotives. It just happened that his first line had that gauge and he had continued to use it. Brunel, on the other hand, had given great consideration of how to build the best possible railway for express trains connecting major cities. It could well be argued that we would all have been better off with travel on broad gauge, but there was one inescapable fact. There was far more of the network built to the Stephenson gauge than there was to Brunel's. It was also true that, while it would be comparatively simple, if it seemed necessary in the future to replace the broad gauge, it would be ruinously expensive to expand the standard gauge. A wider track bed would be needed, with all that entailed in expanding cuttings, embankments and tunnels and widening bridges.

Locke also considered the possibility put forward by the Great Western of having a mixed gauge, in other words a third rail could be laid in between the broad gauge lines, so that routes could be used by both types of traffic. He was not enthusiastic about the idea. His argument was simple: why incur the cost of a mixed gauge at all? Simply prevent the broad gauge being laid instead. 'That there is an evil in the break of gauge is now admitted, and the mixed gauge is put forward to lessen it; but it is evident that the further you push the one gauge into the district of the other, the greater will be the number of breaks, and the greater will be the evil.' His arguments may have been sound, but the government took no notice. In time the mixed gauge was adopted but not for long. In 1892, the very last of the broad gauge was lifted. As Locke had prophesied a great deal of money had been spent on the expedient but to little purpose in the long term.

There was to be one other disagreement with Brunel. The idea for an atmospheric railway had been around since 1810, but nothing happened until the grandly named, but actually very minor railway, the Birmingham, Bristol & Thames Junction, tried an experiment with Mr Clegg's 'Pneumatic Railway', an idea developed by Clegg and improved by two brothers, Jacob and Joseph Samuda. A short length of track was laid in West London in 1840. The power was supplied by means of a small stationary steam engine, which was used to exhaust the air ahead of a piston in a tube, which would then be pushed along by atmospheric pressure. A flange on top of the piston protruded through a slit in the top of the tube, kept sealed by a leather flap. Various engineers were invited to view the experiment. George Stephenson declared it to be 'a great humbug' and Locke was equally unimpressed. Brunel, however, was very taken with the idea, and later decided to use it on the planned extension of the Great Western towards Plymouth by the South Devon Railway.

When it was time to examine the whole scheme before the Act was passed, opinion among the engineers was divided. Brunel was backed by William Cubitt and Vignoles, but opposed by both George and Robert Stephenson and Locke. The proposed railway would have needed a series of stationary engines to exhaust the tube and Locke and Robert Stephenson had already, quite early in their careers, expressed their views on the shortcomings of any such arrangement in their pamphlet examining their suggested use on the Liverpool & Manchester. Neither of them saw any reason to change their minds now. The witnesses were examined in April 1845 by the House of Commons Committee chaired by Hon. Bingham Baring. Although acknowledging the testimony of Locke and the other engineers who had argued against the adoption of the atmospheric system, they gave it their approval and work began on installing it.

The atmospheric railway had teething problems, but for a time seemed to be working well, with top speeds recorded of almost 70mph. But troubles soon appeared of a catastrophic nature. The leather seal, on which the whole system depended, rapidly disintegrated, scarcely more than a year after the first trains had run. Brunel wisely decided not to attempt remedial work, and had to admit the experiment was a failure. The system was dismantled and the line was run by steam locomotives. Today one of the original pumping houses at Dawlish is virtually all that remains as a reminder of the interesting, but fatally flawed, atmospheric railway. Locke had certainly been correct in arguing against the great Brunel; and it never harms one's reputation to be on the right side of an argument. Locke, meanwhile, had many projects of his own that demanded his full attention.

The speed at which railways spread across Europe varied greatly from country to country. In Spain development was hindered by the political situation. When Ferdinand VII died in 1833 he had decreed that the succession should pass to his daughter, but as she was still an infant, his fourth wife, Maria Cristina, would act as the Regent. She favoured a modest degree of liberalism and reform. There was, however, a powerful section of the community whose motto was 'God, Country and King' and who preferred the old system of autocratic monarchy. They wanted the succession to pass instead to Ferdinand's brother Carlos. As the matter could not be settled by peaceful agreement – which is scarcely surprising since the same argument between autocracy and democracy rumbled on right up to the devastating Civil War of the twentieth century – the two sides took up arms. The first Carlist War lasted from 1833 to 1840 and was not a time when anyone was thinking about railway construction. With the defeat of the Carlist forces an uneasy peace descended on the country and progressive voices were heard demanding modernisation and change. The most obvious candidate for modernisation had to be making a start at developing a railway system.

Rather bizarrely the first steam railway in the Spanish empire was not built in Spain itself but in Cuba in 1837, mainly serving the extensive sugar plantations. It was only in 1845 that a native of Barcelona called Roca who lived in London put forward a proposal for a short line northward from Barcelona to the port of Mataró. He must have been aware that after years of Civil War it was going to be difficult to raise capital in Spain, but he was equally well aware that railways had been built in France with the active co-operation of the London & South Western Railway. He approached the Company and spoke enthusiastically about the economic riches the line would bring and was able to convince the chairman, William Chaplin, and other members of the Board that it was a scheme worth their consideration.

Locke was asked to visit Spain and assess the position, both in regard to how simple the line would be to build and whether or not it was likely to prove profitable. The first question was easily answered as the route lay along the flat coastal plain and would require only minor engineering works: there were mountain streams to cross and one short tunnel. And he was satisfied that it would be commercially successful. Agreement was reached: the cost was estimated at £200,000, half of which Roca was to raise in Spain; the other half would be supplied by English investors. But just as things looked all set to go, there were further rumblings of discontent in Spain, and once again the Carlists began agitating for a change in the monarchy. Hostilities broke out in 1846 in what became known as the Second Carlist War but was little more than a series of local skirmishes.

One decision that was more to do with politics than engineering was the decision to build the lines to a broad gauge, nominally 5ft 6in (1672mm). It was clearly not a gauge Locke would have chosen, but the Spanish government saw it as a defensive measure. France was an old enemy, and with the change in gauge, the French could not bring troops across the border by train. Others have said that the choice was made because it would have allowed larger engines to be used in the mountainous regions of Spain, but that was not an argument that would have held much weight for the man who would build lines over Shap Fell.

The line was duly laid out and work was finally able to get under way in 1847. That was progress of a sort, for other proposed lines in the country had simply fizzled out before anything had been done. Other promoters had called in George Stephenson who set about prospecting a far more ambitious route. The grandly named Royal North of Spain Railway was to link San Sebastian to Bilbao and down through central Spain to Madrid. Nothing came of the scheme for a good many years. It was to be one of the elder Stephenson's last major surveys. The rigours of travelling through Spain, often with no better form of transport than the back of a mule, proved too taxing for a man in his mid-sixties. He developed pleurisy on the way home, and retired to his home, Tapton House in Chesterfield. Meanwhile, Locke was happy to entrust the oversight of the Spanish line to his older brother Joseph's son, William Locke. It must have seemed an ideal opportunity for the young man to win his spurs on a comparatively simple route. It was to turn out to be far more troublesome than anyone had anticipated.

Everything seemed straightforward. The familiar team was working together again, with Locke in overall charge as Chief Engineer and with Brassey as the main contractor, who arrived in Spain with his own navvy army. Joseph Locke took a house in Barcelona for a time to keep an eye on things. But the Carlists had not yet given up hope of changing the political landscape. Devey, in his biography, describes those who operated in the area as 'vagrant freebooters' who were using their support of Carlos as a pretext to 'deprive the traveller of his purse in the name of legitimacy.' They may well have seen themselves as guerrillas waging a just war. Whichever interpretation is correct, they were undoubtedly a real source of trouble for the railway builders.

Problems began when the railway company received a demand for about £1,200, which they said was a tax due to them as the legitimate authority of the country, together with a threat of dire consequences if payment was not made. Not surprisingly, no payment was made and shortly afterwards one of the timber bridges was burned down. This was a nuisance rather than a calamity, but a far more serious event happened shortly afterwards. A band of some 200 men appeared in the district led by a man called Borjes, who appears to have been a mercenary. On this occasion, they stopped a train, ordered the English driver to uncouple the engine and robbed the passengers. They had obviously received some sort of intelligence, as they were asking for Locke and his nephew and were clearly disappointed not to have a chance to kidnap the pair of them.

It seems that the area through which the railway was being constructed had been the haunt of smugglers and brigands, who did not look kindly on its arrival. For the former it brought too many prying eyes into the region, and it severely disrupted the trade of the latter. It is far easier to hold up a horse-drawn coach than it is to stop a railway train. It was not difficult to find recruits to join Borjes in attacking the Company and he soon hit upon a new plan. One of the company employees, called Alexander Floricourt, had the job of train guard for the Barcelona Railway Company and one of his tasks was to collect the money from the different stops along the line and bring it back to headquarters. A band of 100 men descended on Mataró where they found Floricourt in a café. If they had hoped to find him with the money on him they were disappointed, so they decided the next best thing was to take the man himself and demand a ransom.

Floricourt was forced to write to William Locke pleading for the money to be paid. Locke resisted the request on the grounds that if he once gave in, other abductions would follow. He was hopeful, however, that the unfortunate man would be rescued, as there were now large numbers of troops from the legitimate army searching for Borjes and his men. The guerrillas were forced to scatter as the troops scoured the neighbourhood and, in the confusion, Floricourt was able to make his escape after sixteen days in captivity. Borjes eventually also managed to escape, leaving Spain for Italy, where he promptly offered his services to another rebellion in Naples. He was killed there in battle.

The line was opened in 1848. Locke had specified the use of the Crewe locomotives for use on the line. The first locomotive to be delivered from Britain was a 2-2-2 engine *Mataró* and a working replica of the locomotive still runs in Spain. The line was a commercial success, and there was a major increase in railway construction in Spain in the 1950s, helped by legislation that made the country more attractive to foreign investors.

Although Locke was not directly involved again in Spanish railways one of his old and trusted assistants was. Alfred Jee had worked with Locke on some of his most important projects, from the early days on the Grand Junction and on to the vast project of driving the Woodhead tunnel. In 1851 Jee had gone to Spain to survey a line running south from Santander to join the Castile Canal. He moved to Spain to live, learned the language and became a key figure in the development of the railway, not only setting out the line but also organising and designing rolling stock. On the grand opening day, 30 August 1858, Jee was given the honour of driving the engine for the ceremonial run, with his brother joining him on the footplate. Everything was going well until the train set off across an embankment. There was a sudden subsidence, the engine was derailed and rolled down the bank. Alfred was instantly crushed to death and his brother died shortly afterwards in hospital. Locke greatly mourned the loss of his old assistant and the event ended his last, if tenuous, connection with Spain. In the meantime he had been kept busy in other parts of Europe.

The Netherlands was comparatively slow to move into the railway age. They already had a very sophisticated transport system for both passengers and goods, based on the extensive canal network. Canals, however, do have a problem: they freeze over in winter, and there was a dramatic demonstration of how disastrous that could be during the harsh winter of 1844, when nothing could be moved on the system for four months. The idea of railway construction had begun before that with a plan put forward by an army officer, W.A. Bake, who proposed a route from Amsterdam to Cologne via Arnhem. This proved too ambitious and faced strong opposition from the powerful shipping lobby. A little later a more modest plan was proposed for a line from Amsterdam to Rotterdam and that too might have been lost had not the king given it his enthusiastic support. Even then it proved to be only a tentative start when a trial single-track line was laid from Amsterdam to Haarlem. It was modest in length but broad in track with a 1.945 metre gauge. Opened in 1839 it proved sufficiently successful for the more ambitious plans to be taken off the shelf and dusted down. A new company, the Nederlandsche Rhinjsporweg-Maatschappij – the Dutch-Rhenish railway – was formed.

Once again, however, there was felt to be a need for British expertise and capital. A start had been made on the route to Arnhem but only as a single-track line. The Dutch declared that the Arnhem line alone, even in its present state, was returning a profit of four per cent so British investors were definitely interested. Once again Locke was called in to advise in 1851. He was actually very busy at the time so he sent an assistant, MacVeagh, to Holland to assess the situation. On his return early in 1852 he and Locke discussed the whole route. An obvious recommendation was that the system should be converted to what was now accepted as the standard gauge, which made a great deal of sense as one of the original objectives had been to create a link with Germany, where tracks had already been built to the 4ft 8½in gauge. This suggestion was accepted for the route to Arnhem. Locke reported favourably on the project, which presented few technical problems, crossing the flat landscape of Holland, apart from a crossing of the River IJssel at Arnhem for which Locke and MacVeagh produced the design for the bridge.

Work began in 1852 with Brassey as contractor and Locke as

consulting engineer. Although everything should have been straightforward, there were some disagreements between Brassey and the Company, which were eventually sorted out. Locke himself made just one visit to inspect the works in 1854 and the whole route was eventually opened in 1856, following the conversion of the Arnhem line to standard gauge. Although Locke's reputation had been an essential factor in persuading investors to look at the line, he played only a minor role in its construction. He was far more actively involved in his other major European project, the Paris, Mantes and Cherbourg Railway.

Successive French rulers had considered the necessity of a naval base at Cherbourg that would help to protect the seaways between their country and the old enemy, Britain. It seemed the ideal spot from which to cover traffic moving from the English Channel out into the Atlantic and possibly attacking important ports such as La Rochelle and Bordeaux. Over the centuries, fortifications were erected, allowed to fall into ruin and rebuilt, and harbour walls were constructed. The most important works were begun under Louis XVI at the end of the eighteenth century, continued under Napoleon I and eventually completed during the reign of Napoleon III. It was then decided that the next obvious step was to connect the completed naval base and fortress to the capital by rail. It is a curious fact that the fortifications first considered as a defence against Perfidious Albion would be linked to Paris by a company with British backing. But it was still the case that the French found it necessary to look to Britain for at least part of the finance and also for engineering expertise.

This was a project that was very much led by the government, but was to be built by a private company. As the purely commercial considerations would hardly have justified the project, the government offered a guaranteed four per cent return on the capital investment. A company was formed with Count Chasseloup Laubat as President and with the board made up of half British and half French directors. There were rumblings of patriotic discontent that the work of Chief Engineer was not handed to a Frenchman, but this was a vital line of communication and the decision was taken to entrust the work to the man with the most successful record of railway construction in France, Joseph Locke. Even after his appointment, when work was under way and going well, there were still suggestions being put forward for his replacement. A decisive factor in keeping him in his post was the wholehearted support he received from Napoleon III. This is slightly ironic, as Locke was well known as an opponent of all forms of despotic monarchy.

It was decided to start by completing the line from a junction with the Paris-Rouen Railway at Mantes-la-Jolie, roughly 50km to the west of Paris, as far as Caen. The first part of the line should have been comparatively straightforward through the gently undulating farmlands of Normandy. Leaving the valley of the Seine the line reached a summit at Bréval, which was pierced by an 800-metre-long tunnel. Locke came to inspect the work at the tunnel early in 1853 with Brassey and William Locke. They all entered the tunnel with a small group of workmen holding torches and climbed up scaffolding to inspect the brickwork. The structure suddenly collapsed and all the men fell to the ground. Brassey and William landed safely, but Locke was struck on the leg by a falling beam, causing a double fracture. The engineer was rushed to Rouen and then taken on to Paris for what was thought to be the best possible medical treatment. The doctors examined the leg and declared that the only solution was an amputation. Locke was having none of that and demanded that an English doctor be brought over to examine him. While he was waiting, cold water was played on the leg to prevent infection and the patient was treated with painkillers.

Sir Joseph Olliffe arrived from the British Embassy and, in his opinion, amputation was not necessary. There is no indication of exactly what treatment Locke received, but it was mostly successful. He had a period of convalescence, where he was forced to lie in bed and occupied himself with reading novels. It would be interesting to know what his taste in fiction was, but sadly the information is not available. When he recovered he was able to return to the line in time for the grand opening, but he was left with a slight limp that stayed with him for the rest of his life.

The first part of the line offered few challenges. From Bréval there is a descent down to the valley of the Eure, which is crossed, followed by a deep cutting taking the line to Evreux. Altogether there were to be five summits between Mantes and Caen, one of which at Lamotte, west of Lisieux was cut through by a 2,500-metre-long tunnel and a steep section with a gradient of 1 in 100. At Mézidon, a branch line ran south to Le Mans, also engineered by Locke.

Once Caen had been reached in 1855, the network of lines linking it to Paris, Rouen and Le Havre were amalgamated into the Compagnie de l'Ouest. As a result of the expansion a new station was completed in Paris, La Gare Montparnasse. The station is famous for an accident in the 1890s, when a train failed to stop and the engine crashed through the end of the building and the locomotive plunged down into the street. The next section to Cherbourg presented a far greater challenge. Much of the ground proved to be very boggy and in the worst sections there was great difficulty in constructing embankments, which tended to sink until they rested on more solid foundations. At one spot the firm ground was only found twenty-two metres below the surface. Elsewhere, cuttings had to be blasted through solid rock. Devey supplied statistics of the work required on the 131-kilometre line from Caen to Cherbourg: 20 million cubic yards of material was removed in cutting and embanking; 70 rivers and 310 roads had to be bridged. The line eventually reached Cherbourg in 1857, where it had a terminus at the arsenal.

The opening was a very grand affair, attended by leading figures from many European countries. Grandstands were erected, covered in bunting and a dais erected with a crucifix for the blessing of the project. Plants and shrubs were laid out, flags fluttered and masts were erected, hung with garlands of flowers. There were bands and parades of soldiers. The Emperor was enthroned, speeches were made – though apparently mercifully brief. Queen Victoria arrived in the harbour on the royal yacht, *Victoria and Albert*. Under a brilliant blue sky and a baking hot sun that left many of the spectators on the open grandstands wishing everyone would hurry up and release them from the furnace, the grand finale was enacted: the blessing of the line. The Bishop in full regalia sprinkled the two waiting locomotives with holy water, recited appropriate prayers and the line was officially declared open. The next day there was a banquet, which Locke attended and where the Emperor awarded him the cross of the Legion of Honour. Brassey reported that at the banquet he sat with the Empress who chatted amicably with him in English.

Brassey was also awarded the cross and his biographer tells an entertaining story about the contractor's attitude to such honours. At a later date, he received the Cross of the Iron Crown from the Emperor of Austria. His agent complimented him on the honour:

Mr. Brassey remarked that, as an Englishman, he did not know what good Crosses were to him; but that he could well imagine how eagerly they were sought after by the subjects of those Governments which gave away Orders in reward for civil services rendered to the State, &c. He added, that in regard to the Cross of the Iron Crown, it had been graciously offered to him by the Emperor of Austria, and there was no alternative but to accept this mark of the Sovereign's appreciation of the part he had taken in the construction of public works, however unworthy he was of such a distinction. 'Have I not other Crosses?' said Mr. Brassey. 'Yes,' said his agent; 'I know of two others, the Legion of Honour of France and the Chevaliership of Italy' 'Where are they?' But as this question could not be answered, it was settled that two duplicate crosses should be procured at once (the originals having been mislaid) in order that Mr. Brassey might take them across to Lowndes Square the same evening. 'Mrs. Brassey will be glad to possess all these Crosses.'

It is not recorded whether Locke was equally cavalier in losing track of his various honours nor whether Mrs Locke appreciated them. The completion of the line to Cherbourg also marked the end of Locke's work in continental Europe.

Chapter Thirteen

THE RACE TO THE NORTH

Although in railway history, the phrase 'Race to the North' is usually thought of in terms of the competing east and west coast routes to Scotland vying for the fastest running times in the 1880s, the competition dates back decades before that. The start of the initial race to be first to build connections between London and Scotland has already been described, and the competition did not lessen as new lines were added. Locke had, from the first, been associated with the west coast route, but in 1844 he received an important post with the rival faction: he was appointed Chief Engineer for the Great Northern Railway.

The idea of a direct line from London to York was not new. The first proposal had been made as early as 1827 when the Rennie brothers had looked at the possibility of a line to York through Cambridge, but that had come to nothing. James Walker, who had prepared the report for the Liverpool & Manchester Railway that had recommended the use of fixed engines rather than locomotives, had surveyed one line from London through Norwich, the London & York Railway; while Joseph Gibbs had come up with a more direct route and in 1836 the proposal was formally presented to Parliament as the Great Northern Railway Bill. At this stage in railway history, bills were still fiercely contested and faced by opposition from landowners and a general feeling that there were more railways being suggested than the country would ever need: the Bill was defeated.

By the 1840s, however, the advantages of rail connections were becoming obvious, and areas without lines felt they were losing out on the economic benefits improved transport was bringing to other regions. Those landowners who had opposed Gibbs in the first place now began agitating for a line to be built. A new company was formed and Walker was asked to resurvey the possible route. It was agreed that there was no case for two companies and two routes, so the rival factions were amalgamated as The Great Northern Railway, and on 17 April 1844, the following advertisement appeared in *The Times*:

Great Northern Railway from London to York through Hitchin, Biggleswade, St Neot's, Huntingdon, Stamford, Grantham, Newark, Gainsboro', and Doncaster, joining the Leeds and Selby and York and North Midland Railways near South Milford, with branch lines to Bedford and Lincoln, and a junction with the Manchester and Sheffield Railway.

This railway intersects a very wide and populous district of country which is at present beyond the reach of existing lines, and whose features are remarkably favourable for railway construction.

It will form by far the shortest line from the metropolis to the north of England, Scotland, and the greater part of the manufacturing districts of Yorkshire and Lancashire ...The preliminary surveys just completed prove that this railway and its branches will be easier of execution than any other great line hitherto made.

One thing the announcement made clear was that the proposed line would offer a new threat to the west coast route, with its claim to provide 'the shortest route' to Scotland. The new company did not get off to the best of starts. Walker was a busy man and felt unable to continue with the project now that he had completed his commitment to surveying the line. The obvious replacement would seem to have been Gibbs. Apart from his early survey work along this route, he had experience as Chief Engineer for the modest London & Croydon Railway. The directors, however, seem to have felt that his experience was not really up to the job of supervising what would be the most ambitious main line yet attempted. So they turned instead to Joseph Locke.

This was certainly a time when Locke was as busy as any engineer in Britain and it might have been thought that his first loyalty would have been to the west coast companies, but they were having problems of their own and serious disagreements about future co-operation. There was an existing route from London via Euston and the London & Birmingham Railway as far as Rugby and then continued through Derby. The Grand Junction had the idea that if there was a new more direct route to York, the L & BR route would fall out of use, which might encourage that Company to be more co-operative. They, therefore, gave their blessing to Locke who, in any case, must have been excited at the prospect of taking control over what was then the biggest railway project yet undertaken. He certainly seems to have been in a cheerful mood at this time, as he wrote to Buddicom in France on 27 July 1844, 'nothing new here except Railways and Railway Bills' and adding that 'no one knows whether his own pet scheme may not have every morning as he gets up, a competing line on each side of it. Lincoln is become a most important place. A line from Wakefield to Lincoln, one from Chesterfield to Lincoln, from Nottingham to Lincoln, Cambridge through Lincoln to York, Peterborough through Lincoln.'

His first task was to confirm the best line – though it is clear from the *Times* announcement that the route through the fens was not a serious contender. He went over the ground and in August 1844 produced his report on 'the proposed railway from London to York and Leeds'. He came down firmly in favour of the line through Stamford and Newark instead of the alternative through Peterborough and Lincoln. He also wrote that: 'The terminus in London must be well placed near to King's Cross New Road, a position not inferior, in my opinion, to any in London.' He also indicated that in the flat land at the northern end of the route, costs could be as low as 'ten to twelve thousand pounds a mile', but they would be much more expensive at the southern end, particularly close to London where land prices were high. His report was immediately accepted.

Once agreement had been reached, the directors lost no time in negotiating with other companies in the north of England to make useful connections. They agreed a merger with the Manchester & Leeds Railway, and as the manager of the latter was also the chief promoter of the Wakefield, Lincoln & Boston, they included that in the deal as well. It made a great deal of sense in both economic and engineering terms, and avoided unnecessary duplication of work. Meanwhile, however, the situation was changing in the west. The Grand Junction and the London & Birmingham had settled their differences and were shortly to merge as the London & North Western Railway to continue their drive northwards into Scotland. As far as the Grand Junction was concerned, the Great Northern was no longer a stick with which to beat a rival, but a dangerous competitor – and their principal engineer was about to start working for the enemy.

There is no surviving correspondence with Locke, but on 17 September 1844 he wrote to the Great Northern, submitting his resignation. The reason he gave was that he had not been consulted about the negotiations with the Wakefield, Lincoln & Boston. It was a feeble excuse: there was no reason why the directors should have consulted him about such an arrangement, and there was certainly no rational reason to oppose an arrangement so obviously to the advantage of both parties. There is only one obvious explanation. There were to be two rival routes to the north, and he could not be the servant of two masters. He had chosen to continue where he had started, to the west.

Locke was now able to move onward with the great project he had begun some years earlier, when he had worked on extending lines from Lancaster to Carlisle. Now he could continue over the border to Glasgow and beyond. For once, however, he would also be involved with a major engineering project only indirectly connected with railways. The construction of the Glasgow, Paisley and Greenock Railway had brought new importance and trade to Greenock and there was now an urgent need to improve the harbour facilities. Locke designed a new harbour, adjacent to the East India Harbour, the work of John Rennie and built in 1805, and sharing one pier with the latter. It was a very simple structure, a rectangular basin, enclosing 5½ acres and providing a total length of 2,350ft of quay. It had an open entrance, which allowed for 14ft depth at low tide and 24ft at high tide. The work was undertaken by the team of Brassey, Mackenzie and Stephenson at a total cost of £120,000. The excavated earth was piled up further along the river bank, but all had to be moved again when the site was needed for the Albert Dock. Eventually all the spoil was used to create the foundations for a new esplanade. The opening of the dock on 17 October 1850 was said to have been, according to a contemporary report 'a great municipal affair'. Locke's involvement did not extend much beyond the initial design phase: the work was straightforward and well within the capabilities of such an experienced team of contractors. The engineer was, in any case, heavily involved in a far greater Scottish scheme.

The Grand Junction had always had their eyes set on an eventual expansion into Scotland, with a line from Carlisle to Glasgow. For the time being they were not directly concerned with reaching Edinburgh as there were already plans being laid by another company, the Edinburgh & Glasgow Railway, to link Scotland's premier cities. The question that needed to be answered was where and how the line should be built, and in 1835 they naturally turned to their engineer Joseph Locke and commissioned him to survey likely routes. The most obvious, direct line was the one chosen earlier for the mail-coach route, heading more or less due north through Annandale via Gretna Green, Lockerbie and Beattock. This was an easy route for Locke to inspect as the line would have had to follow very closely that of the existing road, but this had to cross the range of hills known as the Southern Uplands. Even today this is a wild and sparsely populated region. He calculated that between Beattock and Elvanfoot there would be a ten-mile stretch at the alarming gradient of 1 in 75. He looked for an alternative route and found what he was looking for by swinging westward to join the valley of the River Nith through Cumnock to Kilmarnock, where it would turn back east again to reach Glasgow. This was a longer route, but avoided the punishing gradients: the summit level on the Nithdale line was actually nearly 600ft lower than that on the Annandale route. Locke was convinced that the latter would require fixed engines to cope with the extreme gradient, so he recommended the Nithdale route to the Company.

There is always the possibility, when there are two alternative routes under discussion, that whatever the engineer's report might say, there will be factions arguing for each of them. This is exactly what happened here: if there was only going to be one west coast line, then inhabitants of towns along the way and those with special interests would argue for their particular route. As a result nothing was decided and the whole question was left in abeyance for a time, while Locke was kept busy on his many other projects. One party, however, came up with a new and convincing argument. J.J. Hope Johnson, the MP for Dumfriesshire, pointed out that if the Annandale route to Glasgow was followed, it would be possible to branch off this line and head to Edinburgh and beyond. He envisaged a line like a two-pronged fork, with the line initially heading more or less due north, then dividing east and west to serve Scotland's two major cities. This was an enticing prospect as the east coast route was badly held up by the necessity to cross the Tyne at Newcastle. The difficulty was that the river had to be kept open for shipping, so Robert Stephenson had to design a high-level bridge. This remarkable structure still stands, and is unusual in having two decks, one for trains and one for road vehicles. Johnson's plea to take the more direct line was helped by the fact that he had the enthusiastic support of the Annandale estate: having a major landowner on side would be a huge advantage when laying out the track.

Henry Booth, the secretary of the Grand Junction, was sufficiently impressed by the arguments to persuade the Board that they should commission a new survey from 'an engineer of unquestionable eminence'. When the first survey had been carried out, Locke was still very much at the start of his career, but by then his reputation stood far higher, with two major routes to his credit: the Grand Junction and the line from London to Southampton that was almost completed. In 1837, he set off again, this time with the express objective of seeing if the line through Beattock was possible or not. His initial survey had not been encouraging and he tried now to find ways to ease the passage through the hills. His first thoughts were that it would require a continuous gradient of 1 in 93 for ten miles and even that could only be achieved by the construction of considerable earthworks. He later revised his plans to introduce a new route with just seven miles at the slightly easier gradient of 1 in 106. The route itself was the obvious, if somewhat meandering one, north of Beattock, where it clung closely to the line of the River Annan. There were a number of deep cuttings, but no more severe than on many other lines. It is a mark of how well he chose that modern engineers have never found a better route: the present main road and motorway almost exactly parallel Locke's line.

He also had to consider the best route for the line to Edinburgh. His first thought was to leave the main line at Abington and head north east through Biggar, the route of the present A702, but changed his mind and opted instead to start further north at Carstairs. He put his proposals to the Board, but felt that he had to comment on the problems that might arise from the long, steep gradient on the Glasgow line. It has to be remembered that brakings on trains was still comparatively primitive, often relying on the hand brake on the tender and in the guard's van. As J.B. Snell wryly remarked in his book *Mechanical Engineering: Railways* (1971): 'In an emergency, the driver could always throw the engine into reverse, which was a splendid gesture of romantic desperation but had little effect in stopping a train moving at any speed.' Locke made the position clear in his report:

In the descent, however, there is more danger, and this is a question of importance. Perfect machinery, and perfect watchfulness on the part of the attendants, leave no room for apprehension; and, could these be depended upon, the objections to such planes would be materially lessened ...I am anxious that my opinion on this subject should be properly understood, and I will briefly repeat that, although there is no ground for rejection of this line, I would not, in the present state of our information on the general question, pronounce in its favour.

It could scarcely be called a ringing endorsement of the Annandale route, but nevertheless this was the route that was agreed and the route that would be submitted to Parliament. Work, however, was not going to be started for some time. The government was about to become involved in the whole question of railways to Scotland. Gladstone referred to this episode in a speech to the House of Commons in May, 1888:

It is almost ludicrous, to look back upon the infant state of the whole question at that period, when compared with the enormous development it has now attained. The unusual course was adopted by the government of Sir Robert Peel of appointing a commission or a scientific agency to examine the whole question of what ought to be the line of railway into Scotland. The motive was, that as it was known, or firmly believed, to be absolutely impossible that there should ever be more than one railway into Scotland, it was considered, of the highest importance that the best scientific power of the country should be brought to bear on the choice of the line.

The commissioners had to consider not two but four routes: the Annandale and Nithsdale to the west and two to the east, both starting in Newcastle. To describe their deliberations as thorough would be an understatement: they took two years, from 1839 to 1841, to reach a conclusion, by which time the terms of their investigation were already out of date. It had finally been recognised that one line into Scotland was almost certainly inadequate, so when they produced their findings, they offered two conclusions: if only one route was to be chosen it should be through Annandale; if two were needed then they should be Annandale and the line through Berwick to Edinburgh. As soon as the results were in, the Annandale Committee began negotiations with the Grand Junction, but the arguments had not yet been finally settled. The

Nithsdale faction had not given up the fight and both sides canvassed strongly for support. The Annandales had the rather clever idea of naming their route, the Caledonian Railway, which encouraged the Scots to think of it as their line, rather than merely an extension of an English route. After all the bickering, the Annandale route finally went to Parliament in 1845 and became an Act on 31 July.

The line was not entirely straightforward; parts of it were to run over two old mineral lines, the Garnkirk & Glasgow and the Wishaw & Coltness, both of which had to be converted from 4ft 6in gauge. There was also the question of locomotives to be used on the line and where they were to be built. It was decided to open a locomotive works at Greenock and the man in charge would be Robert Sinclair. He was born in London in 1817, where his father was a merchant. He was educated at Charterhouse but decided in his teens that he wanted to be an engineer, and served an apprenticeship at the Greenock shipbuilding firm of Scott, Sinclair. On qualification he served for a time at the Robert Stephenson works before being appointed as an assistant to Buddicom and Allan at Crewe. He went on to join Buddicom again at the new works on the Paris & Rouen Railway, before being brought back to Britain as General Manager of the Glasgow, Paisley & Greenock Railway in 1844, while still only 27-years-old. He proved himself to be a highly competent manager and was seen as an obvious choice for the new post in charge of locomotive construction for the Caledonian. This was excellent news for Locke, who must have played a considerable part in the young man's advancement. It meant that he had a trusted team around him. It almost goes without saying that the construction contract went to Brassey and now the man who would be building the locomotives was very much in the trusted and tried Crewe tradition.

The line was an immense undertaking, being driven for much of the way through difficult terrain and sparsely populated areas. Shortly after the Act was passed, the first sod was ceremonially cut on 11 October 1845 and soon some 20,000 men were at work. Invariably they were regarded with suspicion and even hostility when they arrived in an area. The line passed through Ecclefechan, the birthplace of historian Thomas Carlyle, who was singularly unimpressed by the whole idea of a railway and even less impressed by those who had arrived to build it. He wrote to a friend in August 1846:

The country is greatly in a state of derangement. The harvest, with its black potato fields, no great things, and all roads and lanes overrun with drunken navvies; for our great Caledonian Railway passes in this direction, and all the world here, as everywhere, calculates on getting to Heaven by steam! I have not in my travels seen anything uglier than that disorganic mass of labourers, sunk three-fold deeper in brutality by the three-fold wages they are getting. The Yorkshire and Lancashire men I hear, are reckoned the worst, and not without glad surprise, I find the Irish are the best in point of behaviour. The postmaster tells me several of the poor Irish do regularly apply to him for money drafts and send their earnings home. The English, who eat twice as much beef, consume the residue in whisky, and do not trouble the postmaster.

By 1847 Locke was able to report very satisfactory progress. He had visited Beattock that August and had got a ride on a locomotive back to Carlisle:

The Line from Beattock to Carlisle is now laid, and prodigious efforts have been made by the contractor during the last fortnight when I saw it, in order to have it ready by the end of the month. A few works remain to be finished off but the Road, Ballasting, Bridges (the operational parts of the Line) are well and substantially executed and I have no fear of any examination by the Inspector. You may open the Line whenever you think proper with perfect safety.

The Contractors are now pushing the works so as to open throughout in November next, and I hope it will be in your power to supply them with means *to enable them to do so. It is perfectly practicable, but it will be necessary to use Temporary stations at Glasgow and perhaps at Edinburgh.*

The line to Beattock was duly opened on 10 September and passengers were able to book tickets from London to both Glasgow and Edinburgh. It was not yet, however, quite the speedy journey promised by railway travel. A train left Euston for Carlisle at 8.45 in the evening, arriving at Carlisle at 10 the next morning. The next stage of just under 40 miles to Beattock was something of a crawl, taking two full hours, after which the railway had to be abandoned for horse-drawn coach: travellers finally reached Edinburgh at 6pm and Glasgow at a quarter to eight. It was at least an improvement over the trip by road. The very fastest mail-coach service was recorded leaving London at 8pm on a Friday and arriving at Glasgow at 2pm the following Monday. The line was a success, but its opening was almost marred by what could have been a catastrophic accident. The following day it was discovered that someone had laid a tree across the line at the Esk viaduct. Fortunately it was discovered before the first train of the day arrived, and although the Company put up what was then a massive reward of £100 to find the culprit, no one was ever discovered. By February 1848, the line had been completed to Glasgow and Edinburgh.

The initial service on the run to Beattock was provided by the typical Crewe-type 2-2-2 with 6-foot driving wheels. In spite of the worries expressed by Locke, during these early days on the Caledonian there were no brakes on the engine, only on the tender and on some rolling stock and the guards van. When the whole line was complete, there were clear instructions on how trains should proceed. On approaching the summit, the speed had to be reduced to 10mph and all available hand brakes screwed down tight and the driver was supposed to use the tender brakes to stop at Beattock. As the brakes all too often lost the battle against gravity, alarmed drivers were sometimes known to put their engines into reverse in order not to overshoot the station. The usual result of that manoeuvre was a visit to the workshops to repair the engine.

Whatever problems the 2-2-2s may or may not have had, they continued to be built in large numbers. Between 1847 and 1855, seventy-three locomotives of this class were constructed for passenger traffic, while there were 61 built for freight work, with coupled driving wheels, seventeen as 2-4-0s and 34 as 0-4-2s. There were a small number of other engines built, sometimes as tank engines. In all during this period 152 locomotives were delivered, 97 of them built under Sinclair's supervision at Greenock. The rolling stock was typical of the period, though the third-class carriages had a touch of extra comfort, as they actually had windows with glass in them, but the effect was rather ruined by the fact that as they couldn't be opened, a gap had to be left to allow air in. And in the often crowded conditions of third class, those left standing must have had a very uncomfortable ride as there was only 5ft 6in headroom.

In his letter of August 1847, Locke had written of the need for a temporary station at Glasgow. The situation there was complicated by the existence of earlier lines. The Glasgow, Paisley & Greenock Railway, Locke's first completed route in Scotland, had a terminus south of the Clyde at Bridge Street, where it was joined by an independently constructed railway, the Glasgow, Barrhead & Kilmarnock opened in 1848 and leased to the Caledonian the following year. This was never considered satisfactory as a main-line station, and Locke's original suggestion for the construction of a temporary station was taken up, and built at Buchanan Street, just south of the Clyde. Constructed of wood, it was not exactly a handsome terminus for such an important route, but no one was too concerned, since it was never intended to be permanent. Locke and his associates would no doubt have been astonished to discover that it would remain virtually unchanged right through to the 1930s. Most of the stations on the line were designed by William Tite, who had enjoyed a long association with Locke. He had notable designs for many of the routes put out by the engineer, including the severely classical Nine Elms Station. For Carlisle, however, he opted for the increasingly popular Tudor style, no doubt thinking it more appropriate for a building close to the historic Carlisle Castle. It is a little ironic that Carlisle should have received a station of considerable grandeur when the far more important centre of Glasgow was served by such a mean edifice. Everything about the Carlisle station was grand, right down to the dining room which boasted an immense carved stone fireplace, complete with Latin motto and the date 1848 in Roman numerals.

The completion of the routes linking London to Glasgow and Edinburgh had always been the first objectives of the Caledonian but their ambitions did not end there. They also planned to advance even further north, right up to Aberdeen, but by now Scotland was becoming something of a maze of competing lines and not everything was going well with the Caledonian. In the letter quoted earlier, Locke had underlined the word 'means', perhaps hinting that the Company did not always provide the funds needed for work to proceed smoothly. Indeed, he was later to cite the Caledonian in Parliament as an example of a company that had been authorised to raise funds for construction and then used them for other purposes. The Company got into a bitter argument with the Edinburgh & Glasgow Railway, a company that offered the most direct route between the two destinations, but who had to compete with passenger boats on the Forth & Clyde and Union canals. Instead of playing their trump card – speed – they decided to compete with cut-price tickets, a strategy that brought them to the brink of bankruptcy. The Caledonian decided that this would be the ideal time to join forces with a collapsing company, but negotiations failed. The Company decided to compete with the inter-city traffic by offering a route through Carstairs, which at least gave passengers ample time to enjoy the beauty of the countryside as they wound their way through the Pentland Hills, south of Edinburgh.

Shareholders became increasingly disenchanted with the management based in London, and there was even a proposal put forward that the London & North Western Railway should operate the whole Caledonian system. When this idea was roundly rejected, it was suggested that Brassey might consider setting up a company to take on the task. Brassey was approached and he at once consulted Locke, with the idea of co-operating in the enterprise. They began working out costs and what was likely to be involved in what would be for both of them a very different sort of venture.

In the midst of a barrage of criticism, the London Committee put out a circular setting out the case for their own actions and continued involvement, but in doing so also hinted very strongly that Brassey was taking advantage of the situation to feather his own nest. This might have been an acceptable argument applied to some railway contractors, but not Brassey, a man of strict probity. He responded angrily, writing to the Board and ending the letter: 'I will only say in conclusion that I believe none of my dealings with the Caledonian, or any other Company, will justify the imputation of an attempt at extortion which is so unjustly cast upon me in the circular.'

It is unlikely that either Locke or Brassey were greatly perturbed at not taking the opportunity to help the Caledonian out of its difficulties. In the event, many of the problems were solved by increased investment in Scotland, which effectively moved control of the whole enterprise north of the border. In any case both the engineer and contractor were still heavily engaged in the next major task of extending the whole system. This was complicated by the fact that extension involved buying up a number of earlier mineral lines, not all of which were standard gauge as well as linking together a number of new, additional routes into Glasgow. Locke and Brassey worked together in the construction of the Clydesdale Junction that linked Motherwell to Glasgow, a very simple line to construct, requiring very little in the way of engineering difficulties to overcome, which was opened in 1849. There was a further extension from Garnqueen Junction, near Coatbridge, eastward to Castlecary, on the edge of present-day Cumbernauld.

Another scheme was also being pursued in the 1840s for a line to Perth, which eventually resulted in the formation of the Scottish Central Railway. One of the problems facing the new company was how to gain access to Glasgow and Edinburgh. At first they had hoped to make a junction with the Edinburgh & Glasgow Railway, but when that failed to materialise they reached an agreement with the Caledonian for a junction at Castlecary. Locke and Errington were appointed as engineers for the 46-mile long line. The Scottish lowlands presented rather more problems than the flat lands just south of the Clyde, but nevertheless there were no very steep gradients involved, though there were cuttings and embankments. The Forth had to be crossed near Stirling, but the river did not present the extreme challenge of the more famous bridge built far later north of Edinburgh. Work proceeded steadily but there were hold ups in finishing the Moncrieff tunnel, just outside Perth. The line to Perth was opened in May 1848.

North of Perth, there was more complexity, with the Scottish Midland Junction Railway, authorised in 1845, arrived at Forfar in 1848, where it joined the Arbroath & Forfar Railway, that had been built as a 3ft 9in gauge line in 1839. That led up to Guthrie, where the Aberdeen Railway took over for the rest of the way. Eventually all these different sections would be absorbed into the Caledonian, but when the route from Carlisle to Aberdeen first opened, there was an extraordinary mish-mash of lines. Starting out on the Caledonian, passengers would then pass over the tracks of the Wishaw & Coltness followed by the Monkland & Kirkintilloch, then back to the Caledonian again as far as Castelcary. After that it was the Scottish Central followed by the Scottish Midland Junction, the Newtyle & Coupar Angus, Newtyle & Glamis, then back to the SMJ. completing the journey via the Arbroath & Forfar and the Aberdeen Railway. It is doubtful if a more complex system could be found anywhere else in Britain, yet somehow Joseph Locke had managed to pull all these disparate parts together to create the first railway system to penetrate the north of Scotland: Stephenson's east coast route had just reached Edinburgh by the time Locke's west coast lines had arrived at Aberdeen. It was a triumph for the engineer, an honour which he shared in good measure with his partner John Errington. By now Locke had been established as one of the leading engineers in the country, and not only had his reputation grown, but so too had his bank balance: he was ready to venture into new territories and make the political ambitions he had first considered in Scotland a reality in England.

Chapter Fourteen
THE MEMBER FOR HONITON

Honiton, in Devon, originally developed as a town situated on the Fosse Way, the Roman road that linked Exeter to Lincoln. It was also considered centuries later as a town that would be served by a main-line railway. It had always been intended that the London & South Western line to Exeter would come through that way. The whole idea of a route from London to Exeter, however, became a little less appealing when the GWR beat them to it with their route from Paddington. Nevertheless, Locke would have been taking an interest in the possible line and, on visiting Honiton, he would have found an interestingly attractive town.

Much of the ancient town had been destroyed by fire, which involved extensive rebuilding in the eighteenth century. Even today the town centre is notable for its many fine Georgian buildings. It was also the centre of a thriving lace industry, though one that had not yet been largely mechanised: most of the lace was handmade in surrounding villages. It had a very high reputation for quality and the town was given the honour of making the lace for Queen Victoria's wedding dress. Lace was not, however, the town's main attraction for Locke. The town returned two members to Parliament.

The 1832 Reform Act had removed some of the worst scandals of the outdated Parliamentary system: the so-called rotten boroughs. The most famous example was Old Sarum in Wiltshire, a place that had once been important but had shrunk to a population of just a few scattered cottages and yet elected two members. It lost both seats and several other towns that had dwindled in size were disenfranchised, while others were reduced to returning a single member. Honiton kept its two-member status, though it was hard to justify in terms of population. And in an age when only the better off sections of the population had a vote, here was ample room for the very wealthy to buy their way into Parliament by making sure those who depended on them also voted for them. Locke, who had toyed with finding a Scottish constituency, now saw the chance to achieve his old ambition to become an MP.

In September 1847 the *Devonport Chronicle* carried a speculative news item: 'It is said that Mr. Joseph Locke, the engineer on the London & South Western Company and the Yeovil line, has become the purchaser of the manor of Honiton, including the whole of the borough. The purchase money, it is believed, was about £80,000.'

The story was almost true. Locke had bought the manor, but not the whole borough, just a considerable part of it. There was no grand manor house, simply some 500 acres (200 hectares) of land, largely made up of smallholdings and a few larger properties. He collected rents, but that was not the point of the investment: he was also collecting cast-iron guaranteed votes. He had, in effect, bought his seat in Parliament. The cost was immense, equivalent to some £80 million today. It is a measure both of just how wealthy Locke had become and how very ambitious he must have been to enter Parliament. It was not, of course, all money spent just for that one end: he would have had some return on his investment, but far less than he could have received from other sources. He also felt that with his new position he needed a coat of arms, which was duly authorised by the College of Heralds. The motto '*Mente non marte*' can be roughly translated as 'Mind not Force' or perhaps more colloquially 'Brain not Brawn'. In 1847 he received his reward: he was elected as the Liberal member for Honiton and retained the seat for the rest of his life.

The railway fraternity thought the decision mistaken – although Robert Stephenson had also taken a similar parliamentary path. *Herepath's Journal & Railway Magazine* described standing for Parliament as 'a silly ambition', while the *Railway Times* declared that the House of Commons was 'a place above all others ill-suited to a thoroughly practical man'. Events tended to prove that the *Railway Times* may well have had a point. Although John Francis who wrote a history of English railways, published in 1851 speaks of Locke's 'eloquence of oratory' and that 'he speaks there with much effect', he was less than wholly successful in getting his ideas across.

Although nominally a Liberal, that did not necessarily make him especially liberal in his views, particularly when it came to Parliamentary reform. The 1832 Act had begun the process of making essential changes, but there were still absurd anomalies. The great industrial conurbation that was Birmingham, for example, had a population at that time of roughly 250,000 but returned two MPs, the same as Honiton with a mere 2,500. There was a swelling movement for reform, from the Chartists who wanted a simple one-man-one-vote system, regardless of income and property, to those who wanted more modest changes – especially on dual representation. Locke's views on the subject were made clear by Alfred Austin in his autobiography:

He called himself a Liberal, but the designation represented, in those days, something very different from what it represents in these; and one who sat for what was in effect a 'rotten borough' was not likely to entertain very Radical opinions. Being independent alike of Electors and Ministers, he voted as he pleased, and I remember being with him in the lobby at the time of the Reform Bill, and his being asked casually by Lord Panmure, then Secretary of State for War, if he thought the Bill would pass a second reading, and his replying, 'Not if it depends on my vote.' Very shortly afterwards, the office of Commissioner of the Board of Works became vacant through death, and in ordinary circumstances it would have been offered to him. I need scarcely say it was not.

Austin's view was from first-hand experience, but Devey in his biography suggested that he actually supported the Reform Bill proposed by the Conservative administration. Austin's version seems reasonable – it was the old, if corrupt, system that had got him a seat in the first place – which he could well lose after reform. He was not, it seems, partisan in his politics. His view was that he would support measures that he deemed worthy, no matter which party had proposed them.

'There were cabinets,' he said, 'who passed good measures from expediency and others from principle. Now, he would prefer to have liberal measure from those who had an interior conviction of their worth; who accepted the principles of liberalism as a doctrine; but he was not going to reject liberal measures when offered by men who adopted them from motives of expediency, since he very clearly saw that if he did not get them from that quarter he was not likely in the present position of party to get them at all.'

It is interesting to speculate as to why a man with an immensely successful and lucrative career would want to be a Member of Parliament, especially as his busy life would not have given him many opportunities to attend the House. Two possibilities present themselves. The first is that the boy who had begun his working life as a lowly apprentice and had worked his way, by his own efforts, to the point where he had acquired considerable wealth, now wanted social status. Engineering was still considered by polite society as not quite the occupation for a gentleman – some might argue that it still is – and he wanted the prestige that went with the initials MP after his name. The other, rather more honourable, theory is that he knew from personal experience that Parliament was still too tied to the past and landed gentry and did not represent the new world where the nation's wealth was being created by industry and the huge technological revolution, of which the development of the steam railway was a prime example. We can get some idea of which theory is more likely to be accurate by looking at the causes in which he took an active interest during his years in Parliament.

Locke tended to speak only on subjects on which he had very decided opinions based on personal experience and knowledge. One of the first causes he took up was Sunday railway travel in Scotland. Sunday travel frequently cropped up in discussing railway legislation, with several attempts to persuade the legislature to ban it – and it was even used as an argument against allowing a railway to be built at all. A typical objection to Sunday travel was raised by Dr G.E. Corrie, Master of Jesus College, Cambridge, who wrote to a Cambridge newspaper in 1851 to 'express his pain that they had made arrangements for conveying foreigners and others to Cambridge at such fares as might be likely to tempt persons who, having no regard for Sunday themselves, would inflict their presence on the University on that day of rest.' The arrangements were, he declared, 'as distasteful to the University authorities as they must be offensive to Almighty God and to all right thinking Christians.'

Such arguments seldom had any effect, but things were different in Scotland where Presbyterianism was a strong force and many lines were constructed under Acts which did not allow for any Sunday passenger services. Locke was given leave to introduce a Bill that would force Scots railway companies to add passenger coaches to the mail trains that were already permitted and proposed a penalty of £200 for those who failed to comply. Locke gave various examples of difficulties that had arisen from lack of trains but his main argument was simple. *Hansard* recorded the debate that took place on 25 April 1849 and in Locke's opening address he said: 'The House would bear in mind that it was not calculated by the Bill to enforce the running of any additional trains whatever, but only to oblige railway companies to attach carriages to those they were already compelled to run for Post Office services.' Which sounds reasonable enough, but one of the opponents, Mr Plumptree declared that the 'Bill was really an attempt to make the people irreligious by Act of Parliament.' He appeared to think that passengers were going to be compelled to break the Sabbath, but as Locke pointed out there would be no extra staff compelled to work and only those people who wanted to travel need use the service. In the event, further discussion was put off for six months, which effectively killed the Bill. This was not to be the end of Locke's confrontations with the Sabbatarians. On the last day of May 1850, when the House was poorly attended, largely it seems because many members had taken the day off to go to the races at Ascot, Lord Ashley rushed through a Bill to prevent mail deliveries to provincial towns on Sundays. Locke was one of the leaders of the opposition to this new law, which, he claimed, had actually resulted in more people working on a Sunday than had before – largely due to items such as provincial papers being rushed onto the last trains running on Saturday nights, so that they were being collected on Sundays. He also argued that if it was an evil for mail to be delivered on Sundays, why should this not apply to all workers? And he asked, rather slyly, whether the servants in Lord Ashley's extensive household were given every Sunday off. It was agreed that the whole matter should be looked at again.

As an engineer he had built much of his reputation on economy and scrupulous costing of all projects, and he was anxious to see Parliament legislate where necessary to ensure everyone was as careful with other people's money as he was. One such question was the misuse of money invested in railways. There were examples of companies raising money by Act of Parliament to build a specific line and then using it to build a quite different route, and the Caledonian Railway had actually used £381,000 intended for construction in buying shares in other companies in the hope of a quick profit. But the 1840s saw a slump in many railway share prices and, as a result, a great deal of money was lost. Various Bills were put forward for establishing an Audit Board to investigate railway company finances. There were two proposed; one would have railway affairs investigated by an external board, the other by an internal audit set up by the companies. Locke supported the second, arguing that 'men who had spent a hundred and twenty million in great public works were fit to be intrusted with the management of their own affairs.' In the event neither Bill succeeded and the whole matter was dropped.

Locke's other concerns largely involved what he saw as a waste of public funds. As an engineer he had always contrived to work within budgets and to get the best possible value he could for the money spent. He did not find the same basic principle being applied in government. He complained about the way in which money was allocated for public works with no proper accountability. He was particularly concerned about money spent by the Admiralty, who seemed not to be required to explain how estimates were reached and how contracts were awarded. His views, it has to be said, were largely ignored. He was also highly critical of the Ordnance Survey, a body that, as its name suggests, was originally set up to provide maps for the military and was still run by army officers. It was, therefore funded by the government. The 1840s were marked by what became known as the Battle of the Scales. Maps were being produced to different scales for Ireland, Scotland and England and it was clear that some sort of uniformity was desirable. Mapping had begun in Ireland at 6 inches to the mile, but as Ireland was regarded as rather inferior to the rest of the United Kingdom by some, it was felt that to uphold the dignity of Scotland, mapping there should be at 24 inch and if Scotland was to get that scale then England could hardly settle for less, yet work there had already begun on the modest one-inch scale. Some now argued that was wholly inadequate and that 12 inches or even 24 inches to the mile would be far better, while yet a third party was calling for a scale that would fit with European practices and proposing 1:2500 as an appropriate measure.

The advocates of the 24-inch mapping saw that as appropriate for surveying, but argued that 12 inches to the mile would be adequate for publication. Locke thought the larger scales were absurd, unnecessary and far too expensive to produce. He sarcastically pointed out that the map of Scotland at the gargantuan scale would be 250 yards long and could only be viewed through a telescope. In dismissing all the larger scales, he was thinking mainly in terms of what he, as a practical engineer, would find useful and argued that the largest scales would only be needed by private landowners who wanted details of their estates – in which case they should pay for their own surveys. There were lengthy discussions, but it was to be years before the whole affair was settled and many committees were to meet to consider the facts and fail to reach conclusions.

Parliamentary speeches in the nineteenth century tended to be long and wordy, but fortunately Locke gave a rather more pithy account of his views in a letter to *The Times* on 26 June 1857 in which he complained that his views and those of Robert Stephenson had been misrepresented. It was quite true that the engineers had explained that large-scale maps would be needed for several purposes but had then voted against the Ordnance Survey printing such maps. He then went on to quote their actual recommendation: 'As regards engraving and publication we do not see any sufficient reason for the Government incurring any expense beyond that entailed in a one-inch map. A facility for making extracts from such a map is what the public would require, but any further expense ought to be borne by the parties requiring this accommodation.' This was written half a dozen years after he had first debated the issue in Parliament, and clearly the matter was still unresolved – and Locke's views on government involvement were still being ignored.

Locke's impact on Parliament was limited: when he argued for estimates to be made transparent he spoke to an almost empty House. He had hoped, as a practical man, to convince Parliament that in its financial dealings and public works it should apply the same strict rules that he would have applied when engineering a railway. He failed. The complex bureaucracy of departments such as the Admiralty was not easily swayed and made to change their ways. He did, however, at least try to raise some important issues, even if he achieved little. It is perhaps worth noting that looking through *The Times* for the years in which he was a Member of Parliament, his name receives few mentions other than to record his voting: none of his speeches were ever recorded at length. It is as well that his reputation rests on his work as an engineer and not on his role as legislator.

He did, however, as a Member have some prestige and influence, and his old hometown of Barnsley hoped to persuade him to use it on their behalf. They were hoping that when the next Parliamentary reforms took place they would be made into an independent borough and gain a Member of Parliament for the first time. Locke replied to their request in February 1859. He was not very encouraging. 'I feel some difficulty in knowing what the Reform Bill is to be', he wrote, 'and I am told the Bill is not yet settled by the Government.' It appears that they had asked Lord Palmerston to act on their behalf, but he seemed to be more interested in Doncaster. Locke agreed that they had a good case, but ended his letter: 'the initiative however must be taken by yourselves.' Barnsley finally became a municipal borough in 1869.

Chapter Fifteen
THE FINAL YEARS

In order to be closer to the House of Commons, Locke had moved to 23 Lowndes Square, just south of St James's Park, London and close to the offices he had opened with Errington. Unfortunately, the house no longer exists, the site now being occupied by a block of flats but still retaining its communal garden that runs the length of the Square. It was an elegant address, a large house with a full complement of servants and certainly very suitable for a successful engineer and politician. He lived here with Phoebe, and their adopted daughter, now officially known as Minna Locke. A niece of Phoebe's, Gertrude Lawrence, came to live with them to keep Minna company and the two girls attended a day school in nearby South Kensington. Phoebe, at this time, was suffering from some form of paralysis according to Alfred Austin, though he gives no further details, but it seems that she was bedridden for some years and not expected to live into old age, though she was to prove rather more resilient than everyone expected. The household was completed by two of Phoebe's relations: her elder sister Sarah McCreedy and a cousin, Eliza Murphy. Presumably they were a great help in caring for the invalid during Locke's absences and there were many of them, for his life was as busy as ever.

As he turned 50, Locke began to turn down many of the jobs he was offered, and although he continued to act as adviser to many companies, the never-ending travels of the Chief Engineer in charge of construction were largely behind him. However, he did have one major scheme that had been many years in the planning, and it took him back to the south of England. Portsmouth had never been really adequately served by its rail links, given its importance as one of the country's most vital naval bases. The original approach from the London & Southampton Railway had been via a branch line from Bishopstoke, and there was an even less direct connection via Chichester to the London, Brighton & South Coast Railway. Now the plan was for a through route to Waterloo, the Portsmouth Direct. The line was opposed by both the London & South Western and the London, Brighton & South Coast railways but

Parliament took the view that a route that reduced the journey between two such important destinations by 20 miles was in the public interest. It was authorised in 1853 and the job of building went, inevitably, to Locke and Brassey.

The biggest problem he faced was the crossing of the South Downs, an unavoidable obstacle, running right across any possible line. He chose to tunnel through at the village of Buriton, just south of Petersfield. It was a major undertaking that involved the construction of a long, deep cutting on the southern approach. From the northern end of the tunnel, there was a 1 in 80 descent to Havant. The opening of the line was slightly delayed by continuing niggling arguments with the London, Brighton & South Coast over running rights, but it was finally opened in 1859. There would be further extensions at a later date, but it was generally agreed that the job had been done well, and at the official opening both engineers and contractor were praised for their efficiency.

Given Locke's continued heavy workload as an engineer, combined with the time spent at Westminster, it is surprising that he found any leisure time at all. He was, however, under no financial restraints as he was far more than merely comfortably off. He had acquired shooting rights on a grouse moor in the Southern Uplands region of Scotland and would often, it seems, try and persuade his colleague, and now good friend, Thomas Brassey to join him. Devey, who had often been with the two of them on these expeditions, gives an amusing account of their very different attitudes to taking time off:

'Why don't you do as I do, Brassey?' he used to say. 'Look at me! I come down here to Moffat, and here I remain for six or seven weeks, and I won't have anything to say to your railways. I ask you to come and stay with me. You come on Monday, and you go away on Wednesday, having tried very hard to get away on Tuesday night, and having spent the whole of Tuesday morning in writing letters; and you know very well that there is not one of them that required writing at all.' 'Well, well, my dear Mr. Locke, I won't write any more letters. But, then, I have my own moor at Roehalion.' Then came more banter:- how Mr. Brassey never went near his moor;- had he ever been there at all?-then it must have been with the intention of running a railway over it.

The story is confirmed by Brassey's son, who described how whenever his father went out on the moor he took a bag of writing materials and letters to answer and, while others demolished the local bird population, he would make himself comfortable in the shelter of a stone wall and get on with his correspondence. Locke and Brassey were not only good friends but also close neighbours in London. Nor was Brassey the only one to join Locke on these shooting expeditions. Robert Stephenson was an occasional visitor, but was more inclined to wander off to study local geology. Locke's nephew, Alfred Austin, was equally unenthusiastic and confessed to preferring scenery to shooting:

The music of the mountain streams, the colour of the glowing heather, the undulations and ravines in the hills, the floating clouds and their skimming shadows on the bracken, these it was that occupied my observation more than the flushing by the dogs of a covey of young grouse or the sudden flutter of an old blackcock, swiftly winging its way down wind.

He sneaked off to write his poetry, but Locke seems not to have minded, as he had always had faith in the young man's ability. Earlier in his life he had given Austin the chance of a partnership in a law firm, but when the young man declined the offer, he simply told him he had probably made the right choice. And when he saw him writing instead of shooting, he merely remarked that he expected 'great things' from him. Austin did at least show an interest in some aspects of his uncle's hobby, writing in some detail about Locke's excitement at being able to replace his old muzzle-loaded gun with a new breech-loading rifle. Locke was, according to Devey, a skilled and patient stalker of his game, but at the end of the day it was back to the hotel at Moffat, where he would enjoy a hearty meal and several tots of the malt. He would then burst into song, 'with his usual disregard of rhythm' but with 'fervour and sweetness of voice.'

The only other leisure activity we hear of is his love of literature. We know that when he was convalescing after his broken leg, he read novels, but he seems to have preferred poetry for his everyday reading, which may help to explain his willingness to help young Austin further his career. In the course of a discussion of how France should be treated, he quoted lines from Byron's *Ode* written at the time of the Napoleonic wars:

Oh! Shame to thee, land of the Gaul,
Oh! Shame to thy children and thee!

One of the guests expressed some surprise at his remembering poems, and Locke announced that he always carried a copy of Byron with him, and then went on to show his latest reading matter, a translation of Dante. He enthused over Byron's lines 'Splendid' he said 'they're magnificent and not more magnificent than true.' The man who had done so much to move France into the railway age and had been honoured for his work had clearly lost his enthusiasm for that country.

Robert Stephenson had, in his latter years, like Locke, preferred to limit himself to consultancy work, of which there was more than enough to keep him busy. His form of escape was to take to his yacht: he was to have two vessels, both named *Titania* and both built by John Scott Russell, the builder of Brunel's massive ship, the *Great Eastern*. The first vessel, built in 1850, caught fire and was replaced by the second in 1853. Stephenson referred to it as his 'house with no knocker', as it was the one place he could go where he would not be visited by others wanting his professional advice. His favourite voyage was to Egypt, and on Christmas Day 1858, he dined in Cairo with his old friend Isambard Brunel. Brunel, it seems, had little time for any form of leisure in his hyperactive life, and the only reason that he was able to join Stephenson was that his doctor had ordered him abroad for a rest and told him to go somewhere warm and sunny for the winter. It was to be their last Christmas together: both men were suffering from nephritis, the kidney disease that can be successfully treated these days, but for which there was no remedy in the nineteenth century. Ill health had forced Stephenson to retire from the Presidency of the Institution of Civil Engineers in 1858, and Locke who had been Vice President took over the position. He must have been well aware that the two great engineers, who he counted as friends were ill, but even so their deaths came as a sad blow.

Brunel, in particular, had been very seriously ill. When the last of his great bridges across the Tamar was completed, there was a grand opening ceremony in May 1859 attended by Prince Albert. But Brunel was too frail to take part in the official ceremony: he was carried across the span on a special platform truck, drawn by one of Gooch's fine broad gauge engines. It was his last visit. He had one other grand venture at that time: what was then the largest steamship ever built, the *Great Eastern*. Its launch had been fraught with difficulty but Brunel was hoping for better news from the maiden voyage: instead all he received was tidings of a disastrous explosion on board. The ship survived the blast, but Brunel's failing strength gave way at the news. He died on 15 September 1859.

That same month, Stephenson was on his yacht, and was himself now seriously ill. After a desperate voyage home, he got back to London only to hear the news that his great friend had just died. Stephenson himself was to follow shortly afterwards, dying in his London home on 12 October. This was an even sadder blow to Locke. The two men had been so close in their early years, working together on the Liverpool & Manchester and, although there had been a rift between them over the Grand Junction, that wound had been healed when Locke rallied to Stephenson's support after the Dee bridge collapse.

Locke was one of the pallbearers at Stephenson's funeral at Westminster Abbey and shortly afterwards he spoke about his two great contemporaries at a meeting of the Civil Engineers. He praised both men for their achievements, starting with a tribute to Brunel and his contribution to railway engineering and ship building. But it was when he came to speak of Stephenson that the address became altogether more personal and emotional: 'Robert Stephenson was the friend of my youth, the companion of my ripening years, a competitor in the race of life: and he was as generous as a competitor as he was firm and faithful as a friend.'

He concluded his speech with comments that were as applicable to himself as to the two friends he was mourning:

It is not my intention at this time to give even an outline of the works achieved by our departed friends. Their lives and labours, however, are before us; and it will be our own fault if we fail to draw from them useful lessons for our own guidance. Man is not perfect, and it is not to be expected that he should always be successful; and, as in the midst of success we sometime learn great truths before unknown to us, so also we often discover in failure the causes that frustrate our best directed efforts. Our two friends may probably form no exception to the general rule; but, judging by the position they had each secured, and by the universal respect and sympathy

*which the public has manifested for their loss, and remembering
the brilliant ingenuity of argument, as well as the more homely
appeals to their own long experience, often heard in this hall, we
are well assured that they have not laboured in vain.*

Locke, however, seemed to be in rude good health. He divided his time
between caring for Phoebe, who by now was unable to travel any great
distances and was confined to a wheelchair, and shooting expeditions in
Scotland. She particularly enjoyed staying at Oatlands Park in
Weybridge. This was a mansion built on the site of the former Oatlands
Palace, which had recently been converted into a hotel. Apparently, one
of her favourite spots was the grotto created there by a former owner,
the Duke of Newcastle, and her husband often took her out for trips
along the Thames towpath. They made one of these happy excursions
in September 1860 but, according to Devey, Phoebe was well aware that
he was missing his excursion up to the moors of Scotland. Like
Stephenson on his yacht, it was here that Locke could get away from
the office and the continuing demands on his time. So he set off for
Moffat in good spirits.

On 16 Sunday he seemed in perfect health, and spent the evening in
conversation with his friends. William Locke was with him at the time,
and when Joseph failed to appear for his usual hearty breakfast, he went
up to his room to enquire if he was well. He was reassured and told to
go out shooting as usual: 'bring home a good bag, and you will find me
downstairs and all right, when you come home to dinner.' But he was
not all right, the local doctor was called and his friends fearing that the
situation was grave sent a telegram to London summoning his regular
doctor. His services were not needed. Locke spent the night in extreme
pain, according to reports, in his bowels. He died the following morning.
The cause of death was given as Iliac Passion, now known as ileus, a
blockage of the intestine. Given the speed with which he deteriorated,
the likeliest explanations are either ischemic colitis, a blood clot in the
artery supplying the gut, or a tumour.

Locke's body was sent by train back to London, following the route
which he himself had engineered over the wild countryside of the
Lowlands and across Shap Fell. A few days later he was buried, at
Phoebe's wish, at Kensal Green cemetery, next to her father John
McCreery and not far from Brunel's grave. Appropriately, the graves of

these two great engineers were close to the lines with which their names were chiefly associated, with the Great Western to one side of the cemetery and the London & North Western on the other. Two years after his death an imposing slab of marble from Aberdeen was placed on his grave, with an inscription that read that it had been 'Erected by his pupils in token of their esteem and affectionate regard.'

John Errington and John Swift were the executors of the will, who each received £500 and there were bequests of £2,000 each to his brothers and sisters, £1,000 each to nephews and nieces, £2,000 each to Sarah McCreery and Eliza Murphy, who had shared his home, and £1,000 to his doctor. The remainder of the estate went to Phoebe and would pass on her death to Minna, their adopted daughter. And it was a considerable estate. Locke had been very successful in his career and when he had made money he had invested it well. Various estimates have been given of just how much he left, but it seems that it was not less than £350,000. In terms of purchasing power that is equivalent to some £30 million at today's values.

Phoebe arranged to make sure that Locke was not forgotten in Barnsley, which he always regarded as his home town, with a number of important bequests. She purchased seventeen acres of land from the Duke of Leeds to create a park for the enjoyment of all the citizens, and Locke Park remains a vital and much loved green space in the town. Barnsley Grammar School received £3,000 for the foundation of Locke scholarships, and although he was not himself a Catholic she gave £1,000 to the local Catholic school and smaller donations to other nonconformist schools.

Statues had been erected in London to both Brunel and Stephenson and Phoebe had the backing of the Institution of Civil Engineers for the erection of a statue to the third of the triumvirate of railway engineers. The Institution employed Baron Carlo Marochetti, an Italian sculptor who was brought up and trained in Paris. Application was made for the statue to be erected in the gardens of St Margaret's, Westminster. This needed the approval of Parliament. They could hardly object to the statue on aesthetic grounds as Marochetti's equestrian statue of Richard I had pride of place in front of the Palace of Westminster. It is possible they thought Locke undeserving, but it is rather more likely that his refusal to toe the party line had made him enemies in Parliament, but whatever the reason, the request was refused. Instead the statue was set up in Locke Gardens in Barnsley, where it still stands today. The statue was formally unveiled by Lord Alfred Paget in January 1866 in a ceremony attended by many of his old friends and associates and the citizens of Barnsley made sure that it literally went off with a bang. The local Corps of Volunteers turned up in force, complete with cannon to fire salvos all round the park. The main speech was delivered by John Fowler, the new President of the Institution of Civil Engineers, who linked Locke with Brunel and Stephenson, declaring that their days were 'the days of giants'. If Phoebe was disappointed that her husband was not remembered in London, she at least had the satisfaction of seeing the respect in which he was held in the town where he grew up. She was to die at the end of that year, and was buried next to her husband. In her will she requested that the portrait of her husband painted by Sir Francis Grant should be bequeathed to the Institution of Civil Engineers where it now hangs in a prominent position.

When Phoebe's sister, Sarah McCreery, died she left a bequest that enabled extra land to be bought that doubled the size of Locke Park. She also had a monument to her sister built in the park. This is a circular tower with a colonnade round the base that fell into disrepair for a time but was fully restored and reopened to the public in 2013. The view from the top of the tower is said to be the finest for miles around. There was one other memorial to Locke, a window in Westminster Abbey, but it was removed and sent up to Barnsley for preservation.

Much of Locke's own work in the latter years had been continued by John Errington, who completed the continuation of the London & South Western Railway to Exeter. It involved several quite severe gradients, and three tunnels of which the longest at Honiton (1,345 yards) proved particularly difficult. He also completed a line from Ingleton through Kirkby Lonsdale and Sedbergh to join the main line south of Shap. Errington died just two years after Locke: the work that had been begun by the partnership was at an end, and with it a vital period of railway history was also concluded.

Chapter Sixteen

EPILOGUE

Locke's obituary, published in volume 20 of the *Proceedings of the Institution of Civil Engineers* ended with these words: 'Thus passed away within a few short months the third of the leaders of the Engineering world – Brunel, Stephenson and Locke:- they were born within two years of each other, and within the same space of time they died.'

This was not the only obituary to link the three names together, yet history has not always been as kind to Locke, giving him rather less attention than his two illustrious contemporaries. It is worth comparing them to gain a more balanced view of Locke's place in the railway pantheon.

There were two major figures in railway history before this trio appeared on the scene. Richard Trevithick has the honour of being the inventor of the railway locomotive and of giving the first public demonstration of its abilities at the famous tests on the Penydarren tramway in 1804. However, he was unable to persuade others to follow in his footsteps nor to invest in his efforts. There was the troublesome problem of the heavy locomotive cracking brittle cast-iron rails, and the engineer's own impatience. He made the effort to make his case, but when no one seemed that interested he simply moved on to other things. A number of engineers, starting with Blenkinsop and Murray, came along at a later date and began the development of the locomotive. But it was George Stephenson who had the vision to see that railways could be something more than merely a means of transporting coal from a colliery to a navigable waterway for shipment. He did not personally contribute any striking new developments to the locomotive, but he was Chief Engineer for the first really modern railway, the Liverpol & Manchester, even if his organisational abilities were a good deal less than perfect.

Of the three men who carried the railway age forward and, in effect, formed the foundations of the modern railway system, not just in this country but who also helped to spread rails around the world, there is no doubt where the popular vote would go. Brunel has always been a great favourite of the British public, not just for his many achievements but also in good measure through his personality. He is the immediately recognisable figure, with stovepipe hat, big cigar and wrinkled trousers. He is the engineer who went his own way regardless of what alleged experts advised. But it is a mistake to overestimate his importance when looked at purely in terms of railway development.

There is no denying that the Great Western Railway route from Bristol to London represented a civil engineering triumph, in offering level, smooth running between two great cities. Had it been built a few years earlier it might have set the standard to which future lines would have been built. But coming when it did, there was never a realistic chance that, whatever the benefits of broad gauge might be, it would supplant the rapidly developing network of lines built to the Stephenson gauge. It was not just in deciding that broad gauge was best that Brunel showed his independence; he built the lines using a very rigid system of sleepers, longitudinal balks of timber beneath the rails rigidly held together by ties. The argument was that such a system would be far more solidly reliable than any alternative. The trouble was that it proved, if anything, too solid, with little or no give. It was not widely adopted. When it came to locomotives, had Brunel's specifications that he laid down at the start been strictly adhered to, he would have had a disaster on his hands. Fortunately, he had the young Daniel Gooch at his side to design what proved to be fast and reliable locomotives. The GWR had its outstanding structures: the wide, elegant arches of the Maidenhead Bridge and the immense tunnel at Box, later to be joined by his last great work, the bridge across the Tamar at Saltash.

Brunel was never satisfied with simply being one of the crowd, accepting received wisdom. If there was the possibility of doing something new and daring, then he was the man. This approach led to his greatest mistake, the construction of the atmospheric railway, a mistake so massive and expensive it could have cost the career of a lesser man. So his life as a railway engineer is not a story of unsullied success. Had he done nothing else, he would still have been listed among the most important pioneers, but his name might not have become so well known. But he did do something else: he revolutionised the shipbuilding industry. He was the man who envisaged a steamship service across the

Atlantic and built the ships that made it possible. The SS *Great Britain* set a new standard, an iron-hulled ship, driven by a propeller. It is fair to say that his contribution to the maritime world was far greater and of more lasting value than anything he did for the world of railways. Judged purely on his contribution to the railways, Locke was more than his equal.

Robert Stephenson started with the advantage that when he began his working life, his father was already recognised as the leading railway engineer of the age. But Robert was a very different man from his father and his success was won entirely on his own merits. While still a young and relatively inexperienced engineer, he was entrusted with the task of designing an engine to prove the value of the steam locomotive as the most efficient device for moving traffic on railways. He not only rose to the challenge, but in *Rocket* he produced the locomotive that was to contain all the main elements that could be developed in the future: he angled the steam cylinders instead of having them set vertically and he used a multitubular boiler combined with exhaust blast to provide the necessary power. It is true that the boiler was first suggested by Henry Booth and exhaust blast had already been demonstrated by Trevithick, but it was in bringing the different elements together that he showed his progressive thinking. He was to go on to develop the locomotive and, in his Planet class, he designed engines that we can clearly see as precursors of locomotives built decades later.

Stephenson also had his share of civil engineering triumphs, notably his great bridges: the high-level bridge across the Tyne in Newcastle and the Britannia Bridge at the Menai Straits, a design he was to repeat in far more difficult circumstances when he had to bridge the St Lawrence River in Quebec. His designs were innovative and successful, but his career might have ended prematurely had he been officially blamed for the Dee bridge disaster. In spite of that one blot on his record, his story is one of high achievements and certainly earned him a high place in the railway pantheon.

These, then, are the two engineers against which Locke's career can be evaluated. He was not an engineer who created innovative bridges, simply because he never needed to do so. The obituary previously quoted also made that clear: 'His viaducts were of ordinary dimensions, though some of them were admirably constructed. In every case they exactly fitted to the places they occupied.' That hints at Locke's great virtue. He was not a man for ostentation, but what he did he did well with a minimum of fuss.

From the first he showed his faith in the locomotive and its development: the pamphlet he and Robert Stephenson produced was a cogent argument against the use of stationary engines for main-line traffic. And when he was in a position to influence the design of locomotives at the new works at Crewe, he promoted the very sensible policy of having the minimum of different designs and standardisation to make repairs as easy as possible. But it is in the field of civil engineering that he made his greatest contribution. In his early career as an assistant to George Stephenson he was frequently dismayed by the somewhat chaotic way in which contracts were allocated and supervised, and determined that when he was the man in charge he would do things very differently. He developed a reputation for bringing in work on time and on budget: a rare event even today. The costs per mile of a Locke railway were generally considerably lower than those of any comparable line. He managed to achieve this admirable record because of the meticulous preparatory work that he put in. At the end of surveying a route, he had worked out to his own satisfaction exactly what was needed and how much it should cost to provide it. That was the basis on which he awarded contracts. The instructions on what was needed were precise and detailed; the costs carefully worked out and annotated. Contractors might grumble – as it seems Mackenzie did on several occasions – but no one ever lost money carrying out a Locke contract. Inevitably unexpected difficulties sometimes arose, but allowance was duly made. The good relations he established with his contractors was exemplified by his long association with Thomas Brassey, who was not only the first choice for most jobs but remained a personal friend to the end.

Like Robert Stephenson, Locke contributed to overseas development, especially with the lines for which he was responsible in France, and was instrumental in setting up that country's first specialised locomotive works. But it is for his British lines that he will be best remembered. If there is one outstanding aspect of his professional beliefs, it is his conviction that the locomotive would develop rapidly and that in the not too distant future it would comfortably overcome obstacles that had once seemed insurmountable. It was this faith in progress that led him to build lines with such severe gradients in Scotland and at Shap Fell. The locomotives of his time might struggle: in the future engines would make light of the problem. It may all have taken a little longer than he expected, but he would surely be delighted to travel his old lines today behind engines that really do dash up Shap Fell apparently as easily as they cruise down it.

It seems likely that the lack of immediately imposing structures has led to Locke's work not featuring in people's vision of railway history and has resulted in a comparative undervaluing of his work. Yet to contemporaries he was the man to have in charge if what you wanted was a reliable, well-constructed railway that was liable to cost you less than it would have done if entrusted to a different engineer. This was good news for the travelling public and even better news for shareholders.

Much of his working life was spent in developing a route up the west coast into Scotland in direct competition with Stephenson's east coast line. Locke won that particular battle to be the first to cross the border, and the rivalry lived on into the latter part of the century, decades after the death of both engineers. The 'Races to the North' were an attempt to persuade the travelling public that one particular line was far better than the other if you wanted to get to Scotland from London in a hurry. The truth is there was very little difference. The final competitive run was made on 22 August 1895, when the west coast route from London to Aberdeen was completed in 8 hours 32 minutes at an average speed of 63.3mph, while the east coast took 8 hours 38 minutes at an average of 62.3mph. Locke and Stephenson were good friends as well as rivals, and both men would probably have regarded the result as an honourable draw. Was Locke more deserving of honours than Stephenson or should the honours go the other way? The answer seems obvious: like the race to the north it is an honourable draw. Joseph Locke deserves to be remembered in exactly the same way as his contemporaries, Brunel and Stephenson, as one of the nineteenth century's great engineers.

BIBLIOGRAPHY

Austin, Alfred, *Autobiography*, 1890

Bailey, Michael R. (ed.), *Robert Stephenson – The Eminent Engineer*, 2003

Brooke, David (ed.), *The Diary of William Mackenzie*, 2000

Brooke, David, *William Mackenzie: International Railway Builder*, 2004

Burton, Anthony, *The Railway Builders* (2nd edition), 2016

Burton, Anthony, *The Railway Empire* (2nd edition), 2017

Devey, Joseph, *The Life of Joseph Locke*, 1869

Dow, George, *The First Railway between Manchester and Sheffield*, 1945

Drake, James, *Road Book of the Grand Junction and London and Birmingham Railways*, 1839

Helps, Arthur, *Life and Labours of Mr. Brassey*, 1872

Joy, David, *Main Line over Shap*, 1967

Larkin, Edgar J.L. and Larkin, John G., *The Railway Workshops of Britain*, 1988

Measom, George, *The Official Guide to the Lancaster & Carlisle, Edinburgh & Glasgow and Caledonian Railways*, 1859

Morgan, Bryan, *Railways: Civil Engineering*, 1971

Nock, O.S., *The Caledonian Railway*, 1961

Nock, O.S., *The London and North Western Railway*, 1960

Rolt, L.T.C., *George and Robert Stephenson*, 1960

Roscoe, Thomas, *The Book of the Grand Junction*, 1839

Ross, David, *The Caledonian, Scotland's Imperial Railway*, 2013

Webster, N.W., *Joseph Locke: Railway Revolutionary*, 1970

Williams, R.A., *London and South Western Railway Formative Years*, 1968

Index

178 Joseph Locke